To my long time friends
John + Ann

23 September 2020

THE VOID OF NOTHINGNESS

Marcel Fraser

Fraser, Marcel, 1932-
The Void Of Nothingness / Marcel Fraser

ISBN 978-1-329-07392-0
1. Meaning of Life
2. Belief Systems
3. Universe
4. Auto-Biography

To life, because it has to be lived

CONTENTS

INTRODUCTION

This is my third book about journeys. The first, "Alone in the Sierra", led me on many backpacking trips to search for my inner self. The second, "Fleeting Journey", brought me to a personal philosophy of life, as I explored other cultures and lands. In this volume, "The Void Of Nothingness", I ask myself: *What am I doing here – and who is asking in the first place?* Looking back on all these inner journeys reveals that I have not arrived anywhere. But that is no surprise. Woe to the one that arrives at his destination.

Our universal search for meaning usually shepherds us to religion, but often vaults us on to unforeseen philosophies. I was born of a Catholic mother and a Jewish father, confirmed a Lutheran, attended Presbyterian Sunday school, and indoctrinated at a fundamentalist Christian summer camp. I held the highest lay position in my church for years, and conducted the service when the pastor was absent. I married both a Catholic and a Jew – not at the same time! All this was taken in stride, and I went through the rote motions that represent religion for many people today. I wasn't too concerned about the afterlife either; like all young people, I was immortal. Today, near the end of my life, I am an atheist with an agnostic insurance policy.

Some material from my other volumes is expanded here to clarify my current ideas. None of my thoughts are original –

but then nobody's are. We are all immersed and linked in a sea of culture from which we sip as we choose. I studied the bible. I read the philosophers. I delved into science. I quenched my thirst about the mind at the font of Steven Pinker, John Searle, Daniel Dennet, Thomas Nagel and others. For the cosmos and quantum physics, I sipped Brian Greene, Michio Kaku, Fritjof Capra, and Stephen Hawking. But above all, I listened.

I'm sure I will offend some readers with my views on reality, meaning, and God. I can only be true to my own beliefs, which have changed as I evolved, and are sure to change again – but I also respect those readers' views which are different from mine. There are no absolute answers out there.

I   INCUBATION

"Give me the child until he is seven
and I'll give you the man."
St Francis Xavier

The early December flurries tease the window panes, while whirls of wind waltz with the swastika flag dutifully hung outside. The building across the street houses a Gestapo command center, so this banner adds a measure of safety. But I care not, for it is the evening before the 6th and Sankt Nikolaus is overdue. I had thoroughly cleaned my room, polished my shoes, and written the indispensable note reminding him how good I had been all year. I knew he carried a book with all my deeds inscribed – but a little bit of last minute persuasion couldn't hurt. By tradition, he came while children slept, but in our house he always burst through the door to present me with his wares in person. A frightening figure: bishop robes, pastoral staff, white beard, booming voice, and heavy burlap sack over his shoulders. Tonight this Catholic saint was late. Rather, my father was late – my Jewish father at that! In later years, I also learned that the sack Sankt Nikolaus carried formerly held the stale rolls my father used to collect before the baker threw them out. These he would soften every morning in his coffee cup. I think he relished his own frugality and timidness. It set him apart. An antithesis to the munificent and self-assured

Sankt Nikolaus. Yet, though my father came from peasant stock, and had little schooling, he was knowledgeable and perceptive.

There Sankt Nikolaus stood towering over me, his gravel voice vibrating the floor I stood on: "Did I do my homework? Did I help my mother when she asked? Did I clean my room?" I knew his bag had fruits unseen in winter, and nuts, and especially candies. But it also held coal for the bad children. I never got any coal, but I did put some inside my own children's Christmas stockings years later, not just as a prank, but to connect me again with my own childhood.

I never played Sankt Nikolaus, or rather Santa Claus, for my children. But the stockings got filled, and the cookies left out at night were half-eaten, and there was always a clamor on the roof. My children would dash to their mother for protection with both apprehension and expectation. One night, sometime after I snuck down from a snow laden roof, the doorbell rang. There stood Santa Claus with a bag of candies and small gifts. How was I going to explain a second Santa Claus? A good friend doing a good deed.

The real Sankt Nikolaus lived during the 3rd and 4th century in what is now Turkey. Countless legends about him have been spawned, embellished, and transfigured, but many relate to his love and protection of young people. The versions about three destitute girls, for example, range from putting gold in their shoes to save them from a life of prostitution, to resurrecting them from a pickling barrel where they had been butchered to be sold as ham! Because of these legends, the anniversary of his death, around the 6th of December, became a religious feast day, then a secular day of celebration.

Later, the Protestant Revolution in Europe morphed the Catholic Sankt Nikolaus into the *Christkindl*, an angel-like Christ Child – without the coal! In America he mutated into Kris Kringle. In England we got Father Christmas. In the Low Countries, Sankt Nikolaus eroded into Sinter Klass, Santa Klass, and finally Santa Claus. By then, the old bishop's cloak had become a jolly red mantle, and the old bishop had gained quite a bit of weight.

But there was also Krampus, who I happily never met. He was Sankt Nicholaus' satyr-like companion who sometimes accompanied him. Krampus would not only bring coal to bad children, but sometimes stuff the really impish ones into his bag to devour later. I was told he was a shaggy creature with gnarled hideous horns, a gruesome visage, dragging chains and bells, and carrying bundles of twigs for flogging. Once my father threatened to send me to the mountains where Krampus would grab me. I behaved after that.

Ah, but there was more than Sankt Nikolaus and Krampus. In Austria, as in most European countries, the Christmas angel (*Weihnachtsengel/Christkindl*) appears on the eve of the twenty-fourth. She is a messenger of God, belonging to one of the nine orders in the celestial hierarchy – so, it seems that even angels have a pecking order! The complexity of this hierarchy, the rigid chain of command, the reverence accorded to each rank, and the division of labor, could only have been thought up by a species that already had such a system in place in order to rank individual power and avoid internal conflict. Nonetheless, I was more impressed with the presents she brought than her standing. Sankt Nicholaus, after all, had only been a foretaste of the glorious material feast I was to consume this night. I never did figure out how the *Weihnachtsengel* came in through the locked window. But I was always banned from the living room that day, until my parents lead me into a world of glitter, wonder and, especially, gifts.

Getting to the gifts, however, was not that easy. First, I had to navigate flames, dragons, and tribal initiations. I had to be purified by my family's rituals. Only then might I be allowed to partake in the sacred mystery of the Christmas tree rite and the *bescheren*, the formal giving of gifts.

Like so many customs we take to be innocuous, giving gifts is actually rooted in the survival of the species. Gift giving reinforced communal bonds, delineated relationships, demonstrated loyalty, and even signaled superior genes, attracting women to men who would share their resources with them, and attracting men to women who would share their resources with their offspring.

Now the early church, of course, found the practice of giving gifts paganistic and offensive. But they could not stamp it out. So they justified it by linking it to the ultimate gift of all,

Jesus Christ. Many centuries later this simple tradition was transmuted by commercialism. People forgot about the ultimate gift. It was now beneficial to the Gross National Product to spend lavishly, and as a bonus, the giver's status could be measured by the monetary value of the gift (just, incidentally, as it had been with early man). All that was fine with me – after all, it assured that I would receive lots of Christmas gifts.

So here I am this late afternoon, still a long way from the gifts. First, I have to run the gauntlet of the ritual. My mother rules the waves; my father bobs in them and knows enough to stay out of the rip currents. I, on the other hand, get the brunt of the breakers. House cleaning had started early in the morning. Every material object in our apartment was bathed, shampooed, washed, laundered, rinsed, sponged, mopped, wiped, polished, brushed, dusted, and dried. After that, my mother inspected her labors, wetting her right index finger with spittle to pick up any stray dust particles that had survived her onslaught. Today, I often catch my index finger in route to my mouth before a knowing smile stops the compulsion.

We had one of the first electric stoves in our neighborhood. My mother measured happiness with material goods, whose main purpose was to measure status. At any rate, the stove also served a practical purpose; she loved to cook, and she was good at it. This day, every burner held a steaming pot, and the cavernous interior wombed Christmas delights. In the corner of the room, the green-tiled ceramic heater regurgitated the black coal it had eaten, transformed into warm radiance. I often sat on its ledge with my back pressed against its robust chest for solace. Today, however, the gramophone was radiating Christmas spirit. But that was not the reality. The day was ruled by apprehension, tension, stress, and anxiety.

Modern day families have not evolved otherwise. Our feigned holiday intimacy is demanding. We don't grasp that childhood memories of enchanted Christmases are illusions. We become frustrated when reality falls short of our expectations. My mother had not evolved either. Nothing was ever good enough for her. Nothing ever satisfied her. Nothing ever matched the images her mind had crafted. And my father, poor soul, played the game to avoid conflict. There was a formula for everything that holy night – all implemented by rote. One had to be a little bit neurotic to play ones assigned part. Of course, the ritual was of more import than the participants.

So there I stand, strangling in starched clothing, and smothering in the sacrament of the ritual. Every movement and every emotion has to follow the prescribed order, as in a Chinese opera. After all, the happiest of all families, at the happiest of all times, has to be spontaneously spawned. Sitting down, I spot our Christmas carp on the dinner table. And it stares straight back at me. Now a carp is no slight creature. It can range up to 4 feet in length, weigh up to 90 pounds, and if it doesn't smoke or drink, can reach 65 years of age. If that's not enough, it's a fresh-water bottom feeder –

and you know what kind of gook is down there! And lastly, evolution managed to sire a fish that contains more bones and scales than flesh. Unfortunately, baked carp is the traditional Christmas fare in Austria.

Carp was originally found in the Danube in the first century. Later, the Romans farmed the fish in ponds they built. Today, European families buy their carp live and keep it in the bathtub for a few days to flush it clean. Either my mother took a short cut, or I was too traumatized by this creature in my bathtub to recollect.

Dinner was awkward, constrained, and stifling – and the carp didn't help. My mother, dressed in her fineries, always wore bracelets that jangled as she articulated her thoughts with her arms. It helped her get more of the attention she craved. My father and I played our parts with studied wisdom. We were both afraid to spoil the game. We had learned to fake our emotions. Unfortunately, I paid for that skill with many hours of therapy in my adult life. Even today, I excel at reading other people, assimilated from my survival skills as a child.

And now it is time to enter the shrine of the Christmas tree – our living room. The Christmas tree originated with pagans in the Northern Hemisphere. The winter solstice, the longest night of the year, was celebrated with evergreen boughs as a reminder that green would return to earth with the lengthening of the day. Evergreen trees were always an icon of life. In the Christian era, people hung fruit from the branches to evoke the sins of Adam and Eve, then pastry wafers to evoke Christ's sacrificial death. Eventually, they wrapped paper streamers around the tree to symbolize pieces of angel hair. Afterwards, the paper was supplanted with tinsel. Martin Luther supposedly placed the first candles on a Christmas tree after being inspired by the sight of stars playing against the evergreens in the forest.

But I am not interested in all this history. I am pondering if it is worth running the gauntlet to reach the gifts. My father opens the doors and we all go inside. The room is dark, but *Heilige Nacht* plays on the gramophone. The tree is a living organism. Green branches, evocative of Medusa's snakes, seem to infuse the entire room. Candles jewel every outstretched branch, mimicking Moses' burning bush. But the glory is left to the *wunderkerzen*, or sparklers, hanging from the branches. These give off an intense dancing light that transports me to the stars of the cosmos. I freeze in wonder, even though I have experienced this many times before. Finally, my eyes sink to earth and the material gifts that I have crusaded to reach. I spot a tin crimped toy garage. Inside is a tin crimped car. And outside, a tin crimped telephone that releases the car from the tin crimped garage when you lift it off its tin crimped hook. Oh, the good old pre-plastic days!

I always feel as if I'm inside a fish bowl when opening gifts. I am the center of the universe and the entire cosmos is watching to evaluate my emotions. And that is followed by the kisses and hugs that seem so counterfeit to me.

Nowadays, I love to watch people's faces as they hug. Some are pained, some resigned, some jaded, and a very few are thankfully in the moment.

I had a different snag with my first wife. Christmas Eve was just another night in America – perhaps to wrap a few last minute gifts. Santa Claus and all the pageantry played out on Christmas Day, the 25th. And at 5:00 in the morning at that! There's no mystery at that hour. Now I concede that we don't know the real date of the birth of Jesus. Historical estimates range between 7 BC and 2 BC. And the time of year could just as well have been spring as winter. December 25th was probably chosen, as so many other Christian feast days, to dilute a pagan festival day. There are other theories relating to the Annunciation and Mary's gestation period – but enough is enough. I didn't really care on what day Christmas was celebrated, as long as it was at night and it was snowing! So verifiably, the shepherds were tending their flocks *at night*. And, the Star of Bethlehem, often depicted as a comet above the newborn Jesus, certainly shone in the nighttime.

But none of that mattered. This was a battle between my traditions and my ex-wife's traditions. In the end we came to an accommodation. I had my Christmas Eve with candles, firelight, and Santa's filled stockings. She had her Christmas morning with the gifts – and as a bonus I was allowed to sleep until 7:00 AM.

So much for Christmas. The Tooth Fairy is another mystery. A storage space in my house safeguards a box labeled "Souvenirs". It holds treasures such as the cast my youngest daughter, Renée, wore when she broke her leg sledding with me, my GI dog tags, a sermon I once gave in church, the small pebble that got stuck in our 300 foot well that I retrieved, and lipstick kisses from the girls in my primary school smudged on notepaper (I guess we weren't that far behind the current generation after all). I rummaged through this collection a few months ago and found a small make-up set my mother used. There's a compact, a lipstick, and an eyebrow pencil – all carved out of now-yellowed ivory. The compact is chipped and the lipstick case rattles when shaken. I open it to retrieve the chip from the compact that is surely tucked inside. But it is not yellowed ivory I find, it is white enamel. My first tooth! I cannot believe how small it is. Surely the Tooth Fairy put it there after she replaced it with a *Zink Groschen* (now a Euro-cent) under my pillow. I must have been around six.

I don't know if I remember putting that first tooth under my pillow that night, but I have the feeling that I did. Memories are like that. One never knows if what is remembered is real, or a feeling, or a remembrance of what one was told later in life. I do know from experience that if something feels like it happened, it probably did. Losing that first tooth was distressing. Part of my body was missing. Infants have little sense of body image. When water drains out of their bath, they are terrified they will follow. But I already knew my body and knew what was mine!

I don't think our grandchildren will have such delicious memories. They know there's no Tooth Fairy before they even lose their first tooth – too wise and sophisticated with their cell phones, computers, and internet social networks. Social media like Facebook, Twitter, and the several hundred other sites out there are assaulting our intellect, mining our data, and burying us in trivia. Our imagination, our culture, and our heritage are being devastated. I treasure interacting with people, gazing into their eyes, reading facial vocabularies, and hearing the spoken word. It is an ignominy that the internet is robbing us of those intimate encounters.

So what instigated this whole Tooth Fairy affair? Well, to protect against witches of course. In the Middle Ages, witches could target you if they possessed a piece of your body, such as hair, fingernail, or tooth. Thus, people first buried their children's teeth to conceal them, later they hid them in flowerpots and boxes, and eventually they placed them under the child's pillow – out of reach of the witches. Losing that first tooth is frightening for a child, so the myth and the money (switched for the tooth at night), consoles the child. How much money does the Tooth Fairy leave? In my day it was pennies. Unbelievably, there have actually been studies showing that the exchange rate for a tooth has kept up with inflation. But the most intriguing statistic is that in the United States today, the Tooth Fairy leaves an average of $3.00.

That lost tooth is also a rite of passage, and as with any ceremony, different societies have different rites. In French speaking countries the Tooth Fairy is supplanted by a little mouse – in parts of Scotland with a white rat. In many Asian countries the tooth is simply thrown onto the roof, or beneath the floor, hoping that it will be replaced by a mouse tooth which grows and stays sharp its entire life. Or, the process is short-circuited and the tooth is given directly to a rodent. Middle Eastern countries throw the tooth into the sky. Japan has rules for throwing the tooth straight up or down – depending. In India it is given to the sun. Africa doesn't do much one way or the other. The Vikings carried teeth into battle, and people have been carrying them as good luck charms for years. The latest fad is shark's teeth on a string.

And then there are all the other fairytales. Where my parents really going to allow the tailor to cut my thumbs off? It says so right there in *"Der Struwwelpeter"* ("The Shaggy Peter", subtitled "Merry Tales and Funny Pictures"). And if any little child missed the implication, there were color illustrations. Merry? Funny? Adults clearly had a weird sense of humor. Sure, the book was published in 1845, but it's still in print today. Purportedly, the stories warn children of the consequences of misbehaving, but do they have to have thumbs cut off for suckling them, burn to death for playing with matches, die for not eating their soup, and be doomed if they go out in a storm, as some of these stories relate? Consider, these stories were written for children as young as three.

I was so captivated by this book as a child, that I recently bought a fresh copy. Gruesome, callous, horrible. Never mind television. This is where violence, anti-social behavior and personality disorders are bred. It's easy to take a child's defenseless psyche and transform the world into a terrifying place to inhabit. A place where one had better hide their deepest feelings. A place where everyone is to be feared. A place where it's better to attack first, just in case.

There are those who believe fairytales show the world as it really is, and it is better to prepare children for that awakening. But very few children need to be prepared to have their toe or heel chopped off, have eyes pecked out by birds, be thrown in a pit of vipers, have lungs and liver eaten, slit the throat of a friend who pretends to be a pig, or dance in red-hot iron shoes until dead. These are the themes of some of our most popular fairy tales – and that's after the critics edited out the darker elements from early editions!

Thousands of years ago folk tales were told around the fire. There were no other diversions. These stories were not only entertaining, but meant to unite the clan, reinforce rituals, serve as forewarnings, and cement social relationships. When the fire gave way to the hearth, the stories passed through many generations and many cultures. The tales explored the meaning of life, death, and myths. The tales were meant for adults, but the children were there too. And nobody worried much about it.

It has been argued that fear, spawned by these tales, teaches children about danger. But there are appropriate levels of fear at appropriate ages, and overt violence is not appropriate at any age. In addition to the violence, many of these tales foster prejudice, anti-Semitism, and racial hatred.

Violence in cinema, television and computer games are as graphic today as the fairy tales of the past. One can evoke violence and fear without being explicit. The imagination is scarier, as those of us who used to listen to radio thrillers can acknowledge. True, such tales and childhood beliefs are ingrained in our genes for survival purposes, and all cultures develop them (just as they develop religion, which is explored later), but we are not doomed to repeat the tales verbatim.

I backpacked with my children when they were young. We mostly went off-trail where there was no one for miles around. We would sit by the campfire at night roasting marshmallows. And that's when they wanted to hear stories. Not any stories, but stories that would frighten them. I had my repertoire, which I varied endlessly, but I always included my children in the list of characters. They loved any tale that had unknown creatures watching our campfire from the deep woods. One night, by chance, there were indeed several set of eyes mirroring the glow of our fire. That story ended very quickly as they ran to their tents for safety.

All children love to be scared. It's instinctual. They know they are not really in danger, yet the experience helps them understand the world and thus survive it. But why do *we* love to scare our children? That's instinctual too. We prepare them for survival in the unsafe world by fantasizing in the safe world. So myths and fairytales do have their purpose (with the gratuitous gore purged). But there is a distinction between telling tales and deceiving our children.

In hindsight, it was a dreadful couch. Royal purple, indigo trim, artless shape – "early cheap-motel". But back then I loved it, although my friends thought it was far too modern. This one day, my older daughter, Brenda, positions a yellow box with red and black lettering lovingly in its middle. All the colors fight. Royal purple, indigo, yellow, red, black. My son, Michael, approaches tentatively and hefts the box. Today is his 10th birthday. It was to be his last.

A Kodak Instamatic 124 camera! Did his sister really give him this? Is he that grown up? Tomorrow morning he is re-entering Massachusetts General Hospital for his third operation battling rhabdomyosarcoma. Nobody ever won that battle then. It has been two years since that ignominious phone call from a bed-side-manner deprived surgeon. "By the way, it wasn't what we thought it was. Your son will be dead within six weeks". It stretched to four years.

So Michael and I have been playing a game of deception all those years. I, that he only has a minor medical problem, and he, that I am telling the truth. Children know. Evolution makes sure they know. Their survival depends on reading their caregiver perfectly. So he fights for his survival while burdened with the fiction. Where is the boundary between fairytales and tales deceiving our children? This was not just my stratagem. The experts at "The General", as Massachusetts General Hospital is affectionately tagged by those who know it well, wrote a paper titled "The Care of the Dying Child", with all the wrong advice.

When one iris differed in size from the other one, the chief oncological pediatrician, who by now was my son's adopted grandfather, told me "he was in the soup". Eventually, he lost consciousness, and the Concord Massachusetts Fire Department brought him from our house to the local hospital. I'll never forget the look of the fireman, a father himself, who carried this forty pound form to the ambulance. I followed to the hospital, but he never regained consciousness. At 2:00 in the morning the phone rang. "Michael has left us". What? He was transferred to another hospital? They lost him somewhere? He skipped out? It took me an hour's worth of seconds to realize what she meant. God damn it! Why couldn't she just have said "Michael died"?

Of course I questioned the existence of God and goodness in the world. I was already quite far down that path. But I had a long history to overcome. As a young child, I kneeled at the side of the bed to pray. Rote words that had no meaning. Eventually, I prayed directly in bed. And finally, I skipped the prayer altogether and just said "Amen" to save time.

When I was the same age as my son was when his destiny was fulfilled, I did not have to rely on fairytales or myths. I was living them. I've penned this before in my volume "Fleeting Journey": the Nazis, the Gestapo smashing the door, *Kristallnacht*, the clandestine visits of that SS man, the night troop train to Berlin, the Jews forced off the plane, our incoming ship torpedoed, the wintry transatlantic crossing on the old slave ship, and my disappearing childhood.

I startled awake. "Christ the Lord is our Savior!" But at 2:00 a.m. in the morning? My five camp bunkmates and I were regularly trumpeted awake at that hour to hear the gospel. The young counselors were fanatical in their beliefs, and compelled to prepare us to receive His grace and salvation as well. I had arrived in New York City as an immigrant the year before, and now had the opportunity to attend a free summer camp for refugees in upstate New York. My parents could not have afforded such things. Of course, the camp was run by a fundamentalist Christian group. This is where I first learned that there is no such thing as a free lunch. I still have the bible I received on my first day there. Bound in black imitation leather with red edged paper, it has a zipper to protect the Scriptures inside. The autographs of some friends from camp are inscribed opposite the title page. Mostly foreign names. The counselors had penned their favorite bible verses as well, all from "John" – 1:12, 21:25, and the celebrated 3:16. But the best treasure was the leaf pressed between the pages of Second Kings 10 and 11. A crab-apple tree leaf, still green after 74 years folded in this bible. There are some that would call this a mystery, but I won't bite. I do remember, however, the orchard of crab-apple trees that a friend and I raided one day, for which we did commode penance for days.

There was prayer at matins, and prayer afore lunch, and prayer before, during, and after dinner, and prayer at vespers. The gaps were filled with bible study. But these were all trivial compared to the 2:00 a.m. salvations in our bunks. All this was meaningless rote to me. But the music at the daily chapel service aroused me towards religious sensibilities. Music was to be my private salvation from this world of suffering and meaninglessness.

In between the supplications were camp chores – including KP. This was actually enjoyable. I remember sitting around with the other boys peeling an endless supply of potatoes. It was a great time to chat and interact while pursuing a common goal. It prepared me for future board-room meetings. One day we received a mechanized potato peeler. Basically, a clothes dryer with a raspy core. Sometimes we left the potatoes in until they ground to the size of peas.

Nothing like the KP I pulled in the army many years hence. Awoken from a cold winter bed an hour later than "salvation hour", I would slosh through the snow and ice to the kitchen which was shrouded in a mist of steam. There I was to clean the grease traps. Huge underground chambers that held the dregs of many meals. It was hard not to add my own bile to the slurry. By the time breakfast was served at 4:30 a.m. I would have none of it.

But camp was not all religious indoctrination. I learned a lot about self-sufficiency, cooperation, and hard work. Those lessons have stood me in good stead to this day. And we had fun too. There was the lake, theater, sports, some crafts, and a clay deposit in the hill behind my cabin. We scooped out the clay and sculpted all kinds of imaginary creatures, which we then baked in the sun to harden. I remember my parent's disbelief when I brought my clothes home in a box, and my suitcase filled with clay dug from that hillside.

Up to now my religious beliefs embraced Santa Claus, Krampus, the Christmas Angel, and perhaps the Tooth Fairy – though I don't know how she ever made that list. As to God – he only existed as a stern father during prayer, who I hoped to cultivate for my future use.

In my early teenage years I attended Presbyterian Sunday school, even though I was formally Lutheran, since the school was closer to our apartment. I never saw my mother at a single Mass, or my father inside a synagogue, though they both gave lip service to their assigned religion – my mother by mouthing a few "Hail Mary's", and my father by eating Matzos on the High Holy Days. I had formed no particular opinion about God yet, but I was absorbing the bible and feeling comfortable at Sunday services. Strange, but I can't remember if my parents accompanied me into the church. As to life, it was eternal – and not in a religious sense. I was just too involved growing up and discovering other people to do any spiritual headwork.

Later I joined the YMCA. It was non-denominational, and any proselytizing was very subtle. I went there to play billiards, using checker pieces as balls. There was also a ping pong table, a small lunch counter, and in a dank deep basement, a pool. I loved to swim there, but for some reason (not found in the Scriptures) you were not allowed to wear a bathing suit. Now that's a pretty tough proposition for any modest pre-teen trying to figure out who he is. I spent a lot of time at the Y because it gave me a place to breathe, unlike my own home.

From here on, all my summers were spent at Y camps, first as a camper, then a counselor in training, and eventually a full counselor. I worked on the waterfront, taught swimming, diving, boating, and canoeing. I must have done something right, because on parent's days, I always received bigger tips than all the other counselors. Yes, there were regular services and short prayers before meals, but no 2:00 a.m. salvation rousings. I got used to religion – it was comfortable and reassuring, but I couldn't really call myself religious yet. Later in life, I sent my own children to Y camps.

Plunging down the New York subway station stairs at Broadway and 110th, I scramble back up on the other side of the street. It was a daily ritual to escape the young thugs who haunted me every day after school. I was a refugee, spoke no real English, wore knickers, and lisped when I talked. Is mob aggression assimilated from elders, or is mankind wired for this behavior. Sadly, I believe we are a tribal society programed for "them and us". And the elders, our caretakers, have not evolved enough to do anything about it.

I sit in the rear of the class, not understanding one word – though several grades above the other children, having had a European kindergarten education. Is it advantageous to learn the multiplication table in kindergarten at the expense of creative play time? It depends on the kind of citizens society wants to produce. But why should society have a voice in the first place? Do we really want to be automatons?

My mother eventually got me into the best prep school in New York, Walt Whitman, on scholarship. She had her ways. I guess I was the token black person. There were only about eight in my class. The teachers were dedicated, and I learned English within a few months – though I still lisped. My best friends were the likes of Tom Dewey Jr. and Paula Vanderbilt. Governor Dewey and his son would pick me up at my house in a limousine to bring me to his farm in upstate New York, while my entire refugee neighborhood gasped in disbelief. My parents even bought a new couch once to receive the governor. When he ran for president in 1944, I was on the campaign stage with him and his son, symbolizing the refugees of the world. By the time he ran again in 1948 I had lost touch with both of them. I did feel a personal connection to the election, however, when he lost to Harry Truman – even though I preferred Truman.

In the same way, the Vanderbilt's chauffer would pick me up to go to Paula's birthday parties at her Fifth Avenue penthouse. Her parents were never there. The maids always ran the affairs. I remember how bizarre it seemed when they served pancakes and sausages as birthday fare. Paula also introduced me to strawberry sodas at the drug store. She would buy them for me, as I never had any money. Strawberry fragments always clogged my straw. And from then on I always ordered those strawberry sodas, until I discovered the famous New York egg creams.

My whole class used to play spin the bottle at school, locked in the bathroom while the teachers pounded on the door. You took off one item of clothing when the bottle pointed at you. As another diversion, we often blindfolded the girls in the basement and kissed them; they had to guess who was doing the kissing. But I never spent a moment thinking about religion, the universe, my mortality, or what it all meant.

On graduation, my home room teacher, Margaret Sherwin, wrote a poem for me which I treasure to this day:

Friedenberg or Fraser
Which shall it be?
Marcel – or – Peter, in the land of the free,
But if you should ask him his real name to tell,
He's sure to reply,
"My name ith Marthel".

Then it was off to the High School of Music and Art, now the Fiorello H. LaGuardia High School of Music & Art and Performing Arts. Then we called it "The Castle on the Hill". Mayor LaGuardia founded that school in 1936, back in the days when Republicans were still on the side of the people. This was the same mayor, who during the 1945 New York newspaper strike, read the comic strips on the air, impersonating all the voices and then moralizing about the meaning of those strips. What a guy!

We used to call them "The Funnies" back then. I also loved reading comic books. They were exciting, easy to read, and helped me learn English. Afterwards, I would separate the binding and divide the paperback into two, then trade each half for a full comic. I guess I had some virtues to learn besides English. Sure, these books are less sophisticated then good literature, but they do have some literary merit.

At school, I found myself surrounded by the top intellectual Jews of New York City, much as today's music schools are saturated with the top intellectual Asians – with only an occasional Caucasian face to be seen. But nobody spoke about their religion or the meaning of life, though we did get both the Christian and Jewish holidays off.

It was hard work, fun work, a full curriculum plus mandatory music and art classes. I already played the piano, but one also had to play an orchestral instrument. So I was assigned the oboe, until my hay fever made an appearance and shunted me to the cello. I had my first crush on a girl,

Louise, and got crushed. I wrote my first orchestral overture titled, of course, "The Castle on the Hill", which was all about Louise. Many composers have done their best work thanks to unrequited love, but that was not the case for me. I look back at that score, now secreted in my basement stores, with embarrassment. Now that I am in requited love, I may try again.

I won a New York State scholarship, a music scholarship to NYU and an engineering scholarship to Syracuse University. I opted for the music scholarship, but my fully "Jewish" Catholic mother gave me a choice between doctor, lawyer, or engineer. I had been taught early on that I was not an individual but merely an extension of my mother. I was only an object or appendage of my caregiver. Fortunately, I processed that with plenty of therapy in my later adult life. But at the time, "I" chose engineering, though music was to be my confidant throughout life.

Scholarships or not, I still had to work myself through school. I delivered telegrams by bicycle, hopeful of those 25 cent tips that would supplement my 75 cent an hour salary. I cleaned houses on the weekends for little old ladies who plied me with lunches and goodies. Looking back, these little old ladies were probably in their late-thirties. It's enlightening to note how we use our own age as an elastic gauge to measure others. I worked in the school cafeteria every night serving food on the line, in return for three meals a day. Feeling sorry for my roommates, I sometimes brought leftover food to them to supplant the Chef Boyardee pasta dishes they heated with hot water in the bathroom sink. And once, four of us took on the job of unloading lumber from a railway freight car. Easy money, we thought. Alas, the timbers were almost as long as the freight car, requiring us to position each one before singly easing them out sideways. We finished half of the car in some 10 hours – and we had to purchase some very expensive lumber-handling gloves in the process. We did, however, amass enough money for a few beers and a great story.

At my first engineering class, the professor asked us to shake hands with the student on our right and on our left, then emoted that one of us wouldn't be here at the end of the semester. He was wrong about the three of us – but right about my playboy roommate.

One of my first life-lessons came from that class. We had to calculate the height at which a catenary, strung between two buildings, would hang. For the mathematically challenged, a catenary is the curve made by a chain of uniform weight suspended freely between two points. The cables of suspension bridges form arcs similar to catenaries. Charitably, the professor permitted us to look up the formulas associated with catenaries. I found the following ones in my reference book:

$$y = a \cosh (x/a) = a/2 \, (e^{x/a} + e^{-x/a})$$

where cosh is the hyperbolic cosine function.

The Whewell equation for the catenary is $\tan \psi = s/a$.

Differentiating gives

$$d\psi/ds = (\cos^2 \psi)/a$$

and eliminating ψ gives the Cesàro equation

$$k = a/(s^2 + a^2).$$

The radius of curvature is then

$$p = a \sec^2 \psi$$

which is the line length normal to the curve and the x-axis.

None of us got it right. Turns out that the chain wasn't even long enough to span the distance between the buildings, so you didn't need any of those equations! Always look for the simple solution. That's the only way nature designs.

At night after homework (usually far past midnight), we would sit around the room with our backs propped against the wall eating ice cream from those now obsolete half-gallon bricks with miniature plastic spoons. Those spoons were never a match for the hard bricks. We discussed women, politics, and religion. But it was man-made religion we debated. No one ever thought about real spirituality or the meaning of life, or the train ride we were all on.

Yes, I was in college, but I was still a child, though I did develop a deeper relationship with religion – or was it just a social thing? Churches and synagogues today are about social relationships, not religion. I'm not personally familiar with belief systems other than Judeo-Christian, though I've been in Hindu and Buddhist temples, Islamic mosques, and Friends (Quaker) meeting houses, but there's no doubt they are all analogous. Sure, there are meaningful moments, and a core of true believers certainly exists. But for the most part, these places of worship operate just like any other social club. There are outings, and picnics, and dinners, and meetings, and study groups, and holiday events, and fairs, and cliques, cliques, cliques. Just no golf.

At any rate I joined the Lutheran Student Association on the main campus. I enjoyed going to the meetings because it gave me an identity, and also because women were there (immature girls, as I recall now). I was shy, and the engineering college I attended was located off university campus in a man-only world. There was one woman in the entire engineering college, and none of us were sure she was really female. Not today, where 20% of the engineering body is female – enough choice for me!

Later, I took a few electives on the main campus. There was time in my schedule for only one elective per semester. Astronomy class got me interested in the sky, but it was just a course in mechanics and Newton's clockwork universe. Nothing about the cosmos or the real meaning of it all.

We already knew the meaning of life back then. It was to graduate into an imposing job, marry a pretty girl, live in a pretty house (prettier than anyone else's), have two pretty children, who gave you pretty grandchildren, who would repeat the same cycle over and over.

Psychology 101 was just another engineering course in disguise. Lots of numbers, graphs, and statistics. But nothing about self-awareness, interaction between individuals, or socialization. Back then, psychology was more about documenting people than understanding people. One of the most influential psychologists of the time, B.F. Skinner, was more interested in studying observable behavior than internal mental processes. He believed that free will was an illusion, and that Pavlovian methods, famously conducted with dogs, was the basis for behaviorism, and the process by which organisms learn. No mind, awareness, or consciousness there.

One year, however, I snuck into the music college and took a semester of piano without telling my mother. To this day I cannot fathom how she tied me into herself so profoundly. She may have felt she had maternal rights, but I think it was more her narcissistic need to extend herself into my being. She had to live her unfulfilled life through me. And I cooperated!

At any rate, the professor told me he wished his music students played Mozart with as much sensitivity as I did. Mozart's own dictum was that the music should flow like oil. And that day I flowed. I still regret that earlier decision to forego music, but I know now that I wasn't a good enough musician, and I never would have had the wide-ranging life I have had. Yet, on reflection, I think we are destined to take a certain life route over which we have little control – not from a perspective of fate, but from a perspective of genetics and physical laws.

II   RELIGION

"With or without religion, good people can behave well
and bad people can do evil;
but for good people to do evil – that takes religion."
Steven Weinberg

The drill sergeant towered over me demanding unending pushups. I had refused to scream "KILL, KILL, KILL, KILL" during bayonet practice. It was bad enough impaling this hapless straw man repeatedly on my callous blade. It was baser to put all civilization and reason aside and let the emotions rule, rather than simply getting the job done. I settled the matter readily. I capitulated, and with wild eyes, sweaty brow, and barred teeth, plunged the bayonet deep into the straw man, screaming louder than anyone "HILL, BILL, MILL, JILL".

Why do we kill, maim, and torture our fellow beings? And why is it pleasurable to some – especially when sanctioned by the tribe (government, armed service, police force, political party, religious organization, clandestine faction). It's certainly not our animalistic brain stem taking charge. It's too primitive to get involved in that kind of stuff. To me, behaving like an animal has always been complimentary – as long as our contiguous evolutionary branch of chimpanzees and gorillas is disregarded. They behave as badly as we. Morality is nascent in most animals, and malice is equally undeveloped. Animals do what they need for survival and nothing more.

So what makes us animals so different? Is it our more developed emotional limbic system, or worse, our highly advanced cerebrum? I can forgive the limbic system – it panics readily. But the recently evolved frontal lobe of the cerebrum is the CEO of the whole mess. It's supposed to plan, organize and guide behavior. Sometimes, though, this wetware corporation, like our commercial corporations, turns into a devious spiritless mechanism and spurts evil for its own satisfaction, with no obvious gain except narcissistic pleasure.

One might argue that pre-wiring of the natal brain, as well as tribal bonds, explain this behavior in complex organisms. But this devious demeanor appears not to add any survival advantage. On the other hand, the irrational unpredictability of such a creature might be a benefit in its interactions with competitors. There's no arguing with a rabid dog that's threatening you. And there's the advantage.

Primates are violent animals, and we are the most aggressive of the bunch. But is there optimism somewhere? A recent study of the muriqui monkeys by the anthropologist Karen Strier suggests that these primates are gentle. She contends that their drive for social cohesion and conformity may be much stronger than their aggression. But will that persist if population density increases and resources decline? Can they evolve? Can we evolve?

There's a delightful yarn by Mark Twain about two padlocked cages. One is packed with animals of different species, the other with humans of different cultures. Both cages are left unattended overnight. The next morning there is nothing left alive in one of those cages. Crowding triggers our aggressive nature. On an isolated mountain trail, or in a small town, I find myself chatting with every stranger. I don't try that in the city.

Any type of life, be it here or on the furthest outreach of our universe, be it based on organic carbon compounds or silicates, be it simple or complex, would follow the same rules – survival of the fittest, or more benignly "natural selection". It's the only way nature works. And we would have the same moral issues with any organisms that had sufficient brain size to permit self–consciousness, as opposed to just awareness. Those are the rules of our universe. Maybe there are other rules, more to my liking, on parallel universes.

I abhor the way the world works. Dog eat dog, might makes right, the law of the jungle, and all those familiar maxims. When natural selection operates on individuals within a group it follows its own rules, and morality is not in the game. Altruism is never rewarded. However, when it acts amid competing groups, altruistic individuals survive because they help the group survive. The fact that there is such a thing as morality, even though it is based on self-interest spawned in the tribal venue, heralds growth. The human mind, with its immense complexity, may evolve in unpredictable directions.

We humans adapt to changes in our environment genetically and culturally. Cultural adaption, stored in brains as opposed to genes, acts faster than biological adaption. Given enough time we adapt to anything – another survival skill, but one that numbs us to violence, breeds callousness to others, and tolerates complacency in ourselves. A recent experience I had at a congested Indian airport proves the rule. There were separate security lines for men and women. I wondered if this addressed modesty or male supremacy. Regardless, I was hastily expedited through the men's line, while the women's line languished. Eventually, the two lines merged at the X-ray screening machine. As soon as I dutifully took my place at the end of that line, full of women as it happened at the time, I was bodily escorted to the front. There, a diminutive woman veiled in black, struggled to place her bag on the conveyer belt. A burly bureaucrat, sharp in his white starched attire, but given the lie by his thong encumbered feet, approached sternly. He quickly exchanged my bag for hers as he admonished "Men First"! Not a single Indian woman flinched. They had adapted to submissiveness. I was not treated as favorably flying to a reassignment during former military service. Ranking only a private, I was now on her side of the line. I too had adapted to submissiveness.

The army, having trained me to impale straw men with cold precision, relocated me to exploit these skills at their premier medical center, Brooke General Hospital at Fort Sam Houston. They anointed me a medical equipment repairman! The first day on the job I was presented with a malfunctioning X-ray machine. I tried yelling "KILL" at it several times – as loud as I could – but the machine just ignored my assaults.

It was a comfortable interlude at the hospital. No one bothered me in my medical whites, and the cafeteria was open 24 hours a day. Every Sunday morning, Christian families would be waiting outside the base gate to take any willing soldier to church with them. Man has an inborn need to proselytize. It's a tribal phenomenon: be one of us, or be our enemy. It delineates the familiar, thus safe, from the alien. And it applies to mundane beliefs as well as spiritual beliefs. After all, if the other shares beliefs, there is no threat to our beliefs.

Curiously, no one ever came by for Shabbat, perhaps because Jews don't advertise as extensively as Christians. At any rate, church was the foretaste. I cherished the communion with God, and briefly felt there was a purpose to the perceived chaos. The "tribe" accepted me as one of their own as I knew their rituals by rote. Their home was my home. After church there was dinner with the family, the proverbial chat around the fireplace, and an outing to a young-adults function sponsored by the church. There were always profuse prim and proper young ladies there to keep one interested. And best of all, the families even let me play with their daughters. At that point in my life, religion had a lot to offer.

It was the same on a holiday in French Polynesia. People there are very generous and hospitable. One Sunday morning, a group of us needing a break from tropical beach-life, decided it would be cool to visit one of the island churches. For the most part, people here still believe in God and go to church regularly. Christianity is the dominant religion, with Protestants surpassing Catholics. British missionaries brought Protestantism in the late 18th century. The French landed with Catholicism in the early 19th century. The unworldly locals were dragged back and forth between the two until the superpowers settled their differences. The French finally established a protectorate, but Protestantism had already rooted. Nonetheless, many villagers still believe in ancestral spirits and found a way to incorporate that into mainstream formalized religion.

So here we were in our Sunday best – such as it was – strolling along banana leaved roads, aiming for the most colorful church to visit. Little by little we were joined by villagers coming from their modest homes following the same track. They too were in their Sunday best, but with a difference. The men mostly dressed in dark trousers topped with white starched shirts. But the *mamas* mimicked peacocks. Bright flowing provincial dresses with clashing blouses and windblown pareos wrapped around waist, shoulder, or neck. Each woman clutched a colorful woven handbag that could hold provision for a week. Oddly, most of their hats were black. But the hues of the parasols that topped this menagerie blinded. Intriguingly, most women remained barefooted, with the occasional thong here and there.

There was already a large group gathered in the shade outside the church. It was their version of our cocktail party with villagers moving among each other swapping chitchat. We, and they, both kept our respective distances, physically and psychically, though each attempted intrusion with veiled glances. When the service started we made sure to sit in the very back of the congregation. No such luck. The pastor welcomed his overseas visitors from the pulpit and bade us to sit in the very first row. The service was mostly in the local Tahitian dialectic with a few sprinkled French terms. Visually, the ritual was a blend of Catholic High Mass and Baptist revival meeting. Afterwards, there was no more reticence. The pastor invited us to return often, and the villagers vied to shake our hands and competed for the biggest smile. Unfortunately, there were no invitations to dinner.

We already know that hell is located right here on earth. But where is heaven located? When I was about six, my maternal grandmother, Antonie, "went away". At least that's what my parents told me. But she never came back. I inherited my hay fever from her. She used to hang wet sheets in the windows to keep out the pollen. Eventually I was told that "she passed". That's such a ridiculous word. Were they afraid to say she died? Were they afraid to admit she no longer existed? They said she was in heaven. I imagined that space soaring up in the sky. But so do the Chinese, and that's in the other direction. Does heaven have a location or is it a state of mind? To me, the concept of heaven is just a refuge from our terrors, a fantasy compensating for our frailties. For some it is a place where souls are united with God. Reunion with friends, lovers, and relatives is a recent fiction. Imagine meeting up with your spouse and lover at the same time. And what age would we all be? Could we choose? For centuries the church has used the concept of heaven to control and intimidate the masses.

Religion is not just about God, it's also about ethnicity. I learned that lesson early. My first serious relationship, after the usual sequence of teenage infatuations, was with Lois, a tall slender Norwegian-like blonde. Paradoxically, she was Jewish. No problem there; I'm a half-Catholic half-Jewish *Mischling*. Eventually, we decided to get married. Attempting to please the families, we struggled between church and synagogue. We compromised with a beautiful hill-top meadow. Her New York socially-aware family would have none of it. I was just not Jewish enough!

Meg, my ex-wife, was Catholic. Her family was devout Boston working class – and it was a large family. I never recalled all those distant uncles and aunts. I attended Catholic services with her, and she attended Lutheran services with me. My pastor had no issues with the relationship, but her priest did. We endured hours of lectures in his office. First he tried to obstruct the union, then he tried to convert me, and finally he settled for a promise that all our children would be raised Catholic. None of that happened. We got married in the Lutheran Church. Meg's grandfather gave her away. Everyone else on her side boycotted the wedding. I was just too Jewish!

Happily, there were no complications with my current wife, Rebecca – a Jew. All our relatives were already dead! Rebecca told me I was the most Jewish husband she ever had. We eloped to Austria and got married at a palace in Salzburg.

So why the universal belief in a supreme power demanding ritualized observances, codified by mankind into religious belief systems? Some give this universal belief as proof of a supreme power. After all, throughout the ages every culture, including tribes never exposed to outside influences, has embraced belief in a supreme power. So there's the proof. Not so!

We humans were hard-wired to seek answers to the unknown. Those answers increased our survival skills and gave us power. So our unconscious mind spewed forth myth, magic, and supernatural phenomena. We began with Naturism – the worship of natural objects that controlled our lives: the Sun, Moon, Rain, Thunder, Wind, Fire, Ocean, River. The list was endless, and these objects all competed for power and for our attention, because they determined whether we lived or died. Then we embraced Animism, the belief that natural objects, including animals, plants, and even inanimate objects have souls that may exist apart from their material bodies. Remember, not too long ago we had "Pet Rocks"? Spiritism, the belief in the existence of nonphysical beings, or spirits, soon followed. That's still with us too! And then we went directly to man-made idols and spawned Idolatry. Here, it is often the physical object, rather than what it might represent, that is being worshiped as a god.

From there it was a short run to the polytheistic religions of Shinto and Mormonism, the henotheistic religion of Hinduism, the nontheistic religions of Buddhism, Confucianism, and Jainism, and the monotheistic religions of Zoroastrianism, Mohammedanism, Judaism, and Christianity, – and now, only half in jest, Capitalism.

Supernatural belief systems were tribal survival mechanisms – and in a sense, still are today. These tribal cohesion practices sired organized religions, which involved a set of rituals and beliefs used in institutional systems of worship. Sometimes the institutions themselves, be they mainstream or eccentric, became the focus of this worship. These institutions spawned early social systems bonding unrelated individuals to each other. This cohesion worked for the mutual benefit and security of the tribe members. Even today, some of the strongest business relationships are shaped through religious relationships. Unfortunately, the same mechanisms that benefited the group nurtured hatred of other groups. Often these mechanisms tend to partition rather than unite. That's not to deny that religion has also brought positive things to this world. But on balance it gets failing grades. It has bred discord, intolerance, and violence. History can sure attest to that!

If religious belief is pre-wired, providing such strong survival advantages, why has natural selection not eradicated atheists? Aside from genetic factors, mutations, and epigenetics, our complex frontal lobe shapes us. True – atheists miss spiritual religious support, and thus are more subject to the meaninglessness of life, which portends lower survival probabilities. But today we live in a multi-dimensional tribal system, simultaneously belonging to many individual tribes categorized by our vocational and avocational interests. And there we get our support.

My father got his support from traditions. Jewish traditions. When he died, my mother gave him an inappropriate Christian burial. At the time I was 32 years old and had two children. Certainly a rational adult. Yet, the dichotomy of the situation never registered until now. Strange! I know my father didn't want to be buried a Christian, but my Catholic mother always got her way. When she died many years later in Arizona, I buried her there. I did not reunite her with my father who was tilling the ground in upstate New York. Looking back, I finally gave my father peace and my mother retribution. I'm sure she wanted to be with him. I had no guilt, no wrath from God, though perhaps from my mother. Had I finally stood up to her?

"The Lord bless thee, and keep thee.
The Lord make his face shine upon thee,
  and be gracious unto thee.
The Lord lift up his countenance upon thee,
  and give thee peace:
In the name of the Father, and of the Son,
  and of the Holy Ghost."

What in god's name am I doing in black robes, mouthing these words to the congregation, whilst palming the air over their heads shadowing a cross? I have become entrenched in religion, not necessarily in spirituality. Here I am, this nice *Mischling* Jewish boy, leading the Lutheran service in the pastor's absence. I am Vice-Chairman of the Church Council, the highest lay position in the church, a respected deacon, apostle of the brotherhood of Andrew and Philip, moderator of the bible study group, and head of every church committee from flowers to finance. No room for spirituality here.

Normally, I arrive at church early and fill the communion glasses with wine – Manischewitz wine, produced under strict Orthodox Rabbinical supervision. Ironically, most Christian churches use this wine, not in the service of interfaith outreach, but because of its relatively low alcohol content. Today though, I remind myself when and where in the service I am prescribed to sit, stand at the lectern, climb the pulpit, kneel at the altar, turn, or bow – and in which direction. I count 21 such episodes.

My voice booms the text of Isaiah 6:8 with authority – lisp, nasal timbre, and foreign accent aside: "Also I heard the voice of the Lord saying: Whom shall I send, and who will go for us? Then I said: Here I am! Send me." I feel power and status as I preach. It's not from God but from man's need for dominium. I sway the masses from the pulpit. With power, mankind controls others and thus resources. With status, others bestow respect and thus resources. It's not comfortable to own those base affects with the rest of humanity.

I pastor the brotherhood of Andrew and Philip as well. The disciple Andrew believed that one could come to belief through the intellect, whereas Philip favored engagement. Either way, their job was to bring the knowledge of Jesus Christ to the masses through personal interaction. And so I roam the Boston suburbs and the rural farms, knocking on doors bearing the gospel. Not much different than what I did when I first got into real estate sales years hence – though the message was not quite the same.

The bunkhouse is right out of John Steinbeck. Single wall salvaged pine boards that don't quite fit together, dust floor pressed hard by untold footfalls, and sheathed tar roof that professes shelter. The clichéd bare light bulb hangs from a rafter by frayed cord. Along the walls, splintered timbers fashion bedsteads. And in the spaces between, wooden shelves made from spent produce crates. The vibrant colors of the crate labels, used as advertising since the 1880's, are the only delight in this functional space – though no one notices but me. These labels not only identified the contents of the crates, but more importantly branded the product, since that was displayed in the same crate in which it was shipped. I peek surreptitiously at the bunkhouse shelves' treasures. I don't want to assault the personal space of these migrant farm workers. But the shelves hold only some meager bags of flour, a few cans of beans, a jar of cooking oil, and a large canvas mystery-bag.

Migrant workers in Massachusetts? I had assumed that was a California thing. And that is part of the problem. No one knows they exist here. In California they are visible, and thus their circumstances improve. These laborers have driven countless miles in battered vans to pick tobacco, blueberries, strawberries, cranberries, and all kinds of truck vegetables. From April through October they follow these crops. Without them our agriculture would not exist. Most are Mexican men, illegal and undocumented, with barely a grade school education. And so, like latter-day slaves, they are often cheated out of their wages, benefits, and basic needs. The human animal takes advantage when it can.

And there I stand, with four years of high school Spanish, trying to make a connection into their alien world. I am more alien to them than they to me. I bring a meager offering: a few cans of corned beef. My congregation has adopted these poor souls, but it's not enough – and it's not suitable. They stare dumbfounded at me, partially from confusion and partially from physical exhaustion. I am embarrassed. What am I doing here?

And then I leave. And then I question. And then I read. And then I reason. And then the fiction of belief by faith alone falls apart. Faith, not being based on proof, cannot accommodate reason. By the time my son is diagnosed with incurable rhabdomyosarcoma I have no more quarrel with God. I spend the better part of a year at the Harvard Medical School library researching the malady. There are no cures yet. The few miracles I find have been misdiagnosed. Every evening I crawl for hours pulling stray weeds from our lawn – my way of extricating the cancer cells from his body one by one. When he dies after four years of suffering, I don't curse God, or question my belief, or pretend that He has a reason for all this. No, God simply does not exist.

So what is the ultimate reality? Well, to the faithful it's obviously God. But without that conviction it's ineffable. I envy the true believers. Their belief matters not, be it theism, idolatry, or satanism, as long as it is prescribed and rote. One does not question and is assured an irrevocable hereafter. Ultimate reality annihilates the bliss of ignorance. Yet, as we comprehend more of the cosmos, multi-dimensionality, quantum effects, and the implication of space-time, our perceptions may inflate as rapidly as the cosmos, and we may approach ever closer to that ultimate truth.

Being a scientist by nature and profession, I know there is no certainty to any premise. And so I become an atheist with an agnostic insurance policy. There may be truth in spirituality, but certainly not in organized religion.

What about spirituality and emotionalism? We tend to get those confused. Well, spirituality abides in the superego where internalizations of rules and morals reside, whereas emotionalism lives in the ego, our selfish nature. The unconscious id, concerned with instincts, is not involved. This psychoanalytic division of the mind, of course, does not correspond to a physical mapping of brain structure. But how to differentiate between spirituality and emotionalism? Spirituality is transcendent and reaches outward. Emotionalism is corporal and within. Furthermore, spirituality incorporates the intellect whereas emotionalism does not.

"Rise up, O men of God!
Have done with lesser things;
Give heart and soul and mind and strength
To serve the King of kings.

Lift high the cross of Christ!
Tread where His feet have trod;
As brothers of the Son of Man,
Rise up, O men of God!"

The massed voices of congregation and choir, supported by the rumblings of the organ, lift me to heavenly bliss. I face the altar, hands raised in literal and figurative surrender, while this music washes over me from behind. It is the end of the worship service and I have sat, stood at the lectern, climbed the pulpit, kneeled at the altar, turned, and bowed the 21 episodes I had reckoned previously. I have triumphed. A strange way to put it. Triumphed in counterfeiting the absent pastor? Triumphed in overcoming my fear of performing? Triumphed in approaching God? Triumphed in giving glory to God? To this day I don't know the real answer.

At the time, I felt a union with God, a feeling that there was a purpose to all this, a sense that mankind was good after all. But was this spirituality or emotionality? I've experienced the same bliss packing alone in the high mountains, listening to music, performing on the piano, or playing cello in a string quartet. Truthfully, I've also experienced this with too much alcohol!

III COSMOS

"We are a way for the cosmos to know itself."
Carl Sagan

I shiver outside the tent and reflect on the warm sleeping bag I just shed – my only comfort in this isolated place. I often spend weeks alone, hiking in the high mountains, just being. It is rewarding to know oneself, and it is comforting to know the place one inhabits. No books are needed. No observations need be made. All one has to do is exist and feel. It's a little like solipsism, which claims that the world, including other minds, might only exist within one's own mind. Similarly, in Plato's famous allegory of the cave, written some 2400 years ago, a group of prisoners are constrained to face the cave wall in front of them. They only see the shadows cast by objects illuminated by a fire. To them, the shadows *are* the reality. Likewise, our image of reality is just a subjective experience of our minds. We believe the illusion is the objective reality itself. There clearly is such a reality out there, unconcerned about us and obeying its own natural laws. But in the end it doesn't matter either way. It's all we will ever be able to know.

But I am cold. A forlorn cold. Like the indifferent cold of space and time. Sleeping at 13,000 feet my lungs have strained at breath. It is the nether of night. Not the comforting night of slumber, but the anguishing night of dread. Night is all we have. The brilliance of sunlight is illusion – the detritus of the atomic furnace inside our paltry star. It can't compete with the vast darkness of space. Overhead, a radiant cloud seems to blanket the sky. But there is no moon to reveal it. My perception fools me. This is no water-vapor cloud, but a cloud of stars – pixels forming an image, the plane of our galaxy, the Milky Way! A hundred billion individual stars melt to form this misperceived cloud. The boundless cosmos doesn't even notice such small numbers.

We can see only a small part of our universe – 93 billion light-years across. Remember, this is a distance not a time. Light can travel around the earth 7½ times in one second, reach the moon in 1 minute, 21 seconds, come from the sun in 8 minutes, 20 seconds, and from our most distant planet, Neptune, in about 4 hours. Imagine how far it travels in 93 billion years! We actually only see out to a distance of 13.8 billion light years in any direction due to the finite age of our universe, but since the universe has been expanding at an increasing rate, those distant objects are now 93 billion light-years apart. The size of the whole universe will forever be unknown. Our observable universe is filled with galaxies, some containing up to trillions of stars confined by gravity. Our relatively small Milky Way galaxy contains only about 100 billion stars. There are over 200 billion other galaxies in our observable universe accounting for some 300 sextillion stars – that's the number 3 with 23 zeros behind it: 300,000,000,000,000,000,000,000. And best of all, there are estimated to be some septillion planets (that's 24 zeros) in our observable universe, with 1 trillion of those potentially habitable. And, we think we're alone? Further, there are countless other universes floating around, all with their own physical laws, multi-dimensions, and space-times. And we fret about mankind's place? Yet, man's mind is vaster than the cosmos and can enclose it, even if it can't comprehend it.

What is space? What is time? Why is there space? Why is there time? Why is there something, rather than nothing? The concept of nothingness has to include no space and no time, not just no "things". Not just emptiness within space, but an absence of space itself. Try to picture no space. It's easy to imagine something with nothing in it. But picture nothing without the something to put it in. As to no time – one can't just visualize a frozen world as in a photograph. Without time there would be no atoms to flesh out objects. Atoms are dynamic entities consisting of sub-atomic wave-particles, and rely on time for their existence. The American philosopher, William James, said: "the non-existence of the world is just as possible as its existence". I'm not convinced. I think quantum effects demand the existence of something.

Ah, quantum effects – that drivel. One who claims to understand quantum physics understands nothing. It's too weird. It must have been conceived by a brilliant idiot. We intuitively know how things work in our macroscopic world. But at the atomic level, nothing follows the rules. Objects can be both particles and waves at the same time – until one looks at them and forces them to make a choice. Not only that, but they aren't in any particular place at any particular time. They exist in a fuzzy haze of probability. Of course, none of this makes any sense in our everyday world. But common sense is not reality. Common sense evolved in a unique miniscule part of our universe – the earth.

The quantum world dictates that whatever can happen, will happen. Heat a pot of water on a stove. It will boil – most of the time. Now and then, try often enough, it will freeze. You may have to wait longer than the current age of our universe, but it will come to pass. Or, take two elementary particles entangled with a common history and place them on opposite sides of the universe. Each exists in a fog of probability without possessing any particular state. Measure one, and the other instantly knows what is happening to its partner. Albert Einstein derided this as "spooky action at a distance". But experiments have consistently shown, spooky or not, that this is exactly what happens. Or, measure some property of an object and you immediately limit your ability to measure a related property (the famous Heisenberg Uncertainty Principal). For example, the more you limit the position of an object (or space-time for that matter), the less you know about its momentum, and the more its velocity and energy can sway. Put simply, one could say that the more you know about the position of a baseball, the less you know about its speed. And it's not because we're poor at measuring. It's because everything in the universe behaves like a particle and a wave at the same time.

So, at extremely small scales of space-time (or even zero space-time), momentum and energy can temporarily become turbulent, resulting in what is called a quantum foam. Virtual bubbles pop in and out of existence in this foam, just as water vapor bubbles do in boiling water – except that these bubbles have 11 space-time dimensions. One of these bubbles may have expanded into a universe such as ours. The bubbles birthed from nothing, each one an entire universe already pregnant with its own universes. The radiation field in these bubbles transformed into equal amounts of matter and anti-matter, which annihilated each other on contact, transforming back to radiation, satisfying our logic of not getting something from nothing. However, it seems that an infinitesimally small excess of matter, as opposed to anti-matter, remained. No one knows why. But the fact that we're here is the ultimate proof.

Some scientists question if external reality, including the entire universe, actually exists if we're not experiencing it. Quantum effects blur the boundary between our subjective reality and the objective reality that's "out there". It's possible that our consciousness and our actions influence the state of the universe, just as they influence the "spooky" entangled particles on opposite sides of the universe. And I hesitate to mention, that similarly, it might be possible to influence that part of the past that has not yet been determined – and that experiments have already proven that possibility. We select the quantum history we choose out of endless possibilities.

Yet, mankind has a predisposition for order and continuity, so we ask: "What was there before nothing?" Of course, that's an irrational question. And if there were something there before nothing, we'd have to answer the question: "How did something turn into nothing?" A more practical question might be: "Why did it take so long for something to come out of nothing?" And that's just as vacuous as all the other queries, because if there was no anything, there was also no time in which to wait.

Are there other universes waiting to be created out of nothing? Probably. Universes are no more unique in the cosmos than man is unique in his universe. One has to ponder the entire cosmos, not just our universe, to comprehend why there is something rather than nothing. Maybe there is always something, but other universes take turns incubating it.

Our universe, created out of nothing, still adds up to nothing, given that the positive energy of all matter (ordinary and dark) perfectly balances the negative energy of all gravity (ordinary and dark). The original quantum foam birthed the bubbles from nothingness – no space, no time. But what spawned the laws of nature, and specifically the laws of quantum mechanics? No one knows. Those laws had to be in place before a quantum foam could exist and birth our universe. So, the only plausible explanation is that those laws were always there. And remember, *always* wasn't that long, because time did not exist before our universe materialized. Do quantum effects apply only to the laws of our universe, not to other universes? No one knows. Where does all this leave us? No one knows. Here, some evoke God for lack of a better retort.

Of course, all this could be wrong. Maybe our universe didn't evolve from nothingness. The most recent ideas imagine an ekpyrotic (Greek for conflagration) universe eternally cycling between fiery birth and glacial death. According to this scenario, our universe lay frozen for an unimaginable number of years until some 14 billion years ago when a parallel universe, hidden in higher dimensions, collided with ours. Energy from this collision transformed into the matter that we know today in our three dimensional universe. Allegedly, there are countless such universes floating around on hidden higher-dimensional planes known as branes. These branes are just multi-dimensional mem*branes* acting as boundaries or walls. An oft-used example is that of a two dimensional bedsheet hanging on a clothesline in a three dimensional world. If beings lived on the bedsheet, they would have no idea that they were immersed in a three dimensional world. We live in that three dimensional world, but the branes around us could have as many as ten spatial-dimensions. We can't sense the other branes because almost everything that exists, including light, is confined to our own brane – except for gravity. And gravity, attracting nearby branes, is what caused the collision in the first place. This interaction between branes may be an alternate explanation for the dark energy considered later in this chapter. For the technical minded, string theory manifests gravity by closed strings or loops, whereas everything else in our universe is manifested by open or cut strings. Open strings have two ends which are stuck to our brane, but gravity's loops are free to float to other branes. This also explains why gravity is so much weaker than the other forces of nature – it leaks to other branes.

Another possibility for a cyclical universe, known as the Big Bounce, visualizes the collapse of a prior universe very similar to ours. This universe never gets infinitesimally small but rebounds to form a new universe. The scenario eliminates the problem of what was there before nothingness, but implies a never-ending cycle of universes. This theory is currently being tested with gravity-wave detectors.

But I am here now, and being here now, I'm apprehensive that I might co-exist in different space-times in this universe. That is, there may be another self (or many selves) somewhere out there now, or in the past, or in the future. The enigma compounds if I live in a multiverse, an infinite number of co-existing universes. I could be living my lives in endless variations. And, what bodily shapes do these selves inhabit, assuming they even have a body? Obviously, I'm not conscious of any of them – but what if those other selves are being burned at the stake right now, or burning others, or are just despondent and cold? I can't feel what they feel, but personally they can and do. And what if they're not quasi-clones but really *are* me?

The laws of classical physics are deterministic. That means if we know exactly how everything is in the universe right now, we could calculate how everything was or will be at any point in time. That also implies that there is no such thing as free will. So, the next word I choose to write here has been predetermined since the beginning of the universe. All previous events that have happened, right up to the electro-chemical signal a synapse in my brain is about to pass to its neighbor, have already determined that word. I have nothing to do with it. Pretty depressing!

Quantum effects to the rescue. At really small space-time scales, one cannot determine the outcome of an event with certainty, only the probability of the outcome. This miniscule probability foam can nevertheless affect the outcome of macro-scale events. Take the oft quoted "butterfly effect" where a butterfly's chosen route past a blade of grass influences one small event after another, in domino fashion, until weather patterns change on the other side of the world. And remember, the butterfly's choice of route was also shaped by quantum effects. On the other hand, this probability foam may simply be an illusion if quantum effects only represent our ignorance of the real equations.

Further, string theory suggests that elementary particles are made of vibrating strings – the nature of the vibration determining the nature of the particles. These strings are on the order of the Planck length, or approximately 1.67×10^{-33} cm. That's a number with 32 zeros after the decimal point: 0.000,000,000,000,000,000,000,000,000,00167 – as small as things can get for us. Our universe is probably infinite but bounded, but we see only an infinitesimal fraction of it, about 5×10^{23} miles across! That's a number with 23 zeros before the decimal point: 500,000,000,000,000,000,000,000.0 – as large as things can get for us. We evolved to understand things at anthropomorphic scales. When we try to imagine such small or large distances, our minds vault to the end, not capable of grasping the entire journey.

It's impossible to make sense of something using a scale different in magnitude from the object under consideration. For example, try to analyze the flight of a bee seeking nectar by analyzing the motion of every single atom in the bee, the flower, and the air it flies in. And to make it simple, let's forget about quantum foam. Sure, given enough computational power we can come up with lots of processed data. But it would tell us nothing of the real event. Similarly, we might do the math of the universe and yet grasp nothing of its truth.

Mankind is not the center of anything, and the stuff we are made of, and everything we know, makes up only some 4.9 percent of what's "out there". And most of that is just hydrogen and helium, leaving a meager 0.1 percent for everything else that we interact with! The rest is this mysterious dark energy and dark matter. We really are the detritus of the cosmos. We are not meant to comprehend the cosmos (with apologies to Carl Sagan's epigraph) – though we try. Only the cosmos comprehends itself. Too much for poor old me.

Right now and always, according to Einstein, *all* of space and *all* of time exist. It's easy to visualize another place that exists at this moment even though we're not there. But try to visualize a different moment in time that exists at *this* moment. That is, visualize a moment in the past or the future that is happening right now! Going to your memory for the past, or your imagination for the future doesn't count. Perhaps this is so difficult for us because we have the wrong concept of what time really is. Einstein once said: "For we convinced physicists, the distinction between past, present, and future is only an illusion, however persistent. The only thing that's real is space-time. Each moment – each event or happening – exists, just as each point in space exists". He believed that reality embraces past, present, and future equally, and that the flow of time we envision bringing one section to light as another goes dark is illusory. Some scholars, agreeing that the past exists in the present, disagree that the future also exists in the present. Others claim that there is no such thing as time; there is only a change in the appearance of our clocks – whether they are mechanical, optical, or atomic.

To me, all of time could exist right now and forever, but only on a theoretical mathematical basis. Whether time flows continuously as a river, or advances frame by frame as a movie, or fully exists at all times as a solid block, time travel as we imagine it wouldn't succeed. When we arrive in the past with our time machine, we would be the person we were in that past, not the person we are today. So we wouldn't be aware of our future, or that we had just stepped out of a time machine. If we went to the future instead, we would be aware of our time travel, as it is in our memory of the past, but on returning we would know nothing of our trip because the person in our present is not the same person that was in the future. If we were somehow able to travel to the past or the future and yet remain in the "present", so to speak, we would only be an observer in those other domains, not a participant.

One must be careful to distinguish between what one senses, and what one imagines as "now". For instance, we "sense" the light of a distant star through our eyes, but know that the light took a long time to reach us. So we reason, correctly, that we are seeing the star how it looked a long time ago, in its past – which is *our* present. However, we can also "imagine" that star as it is right now – in *its* present.

Just like that star, light speeds away from our bodies at, well, the speed of light. If we were able to sprint ahead of that light beam, or just take a shortcut through a wormhole in space, we could watch ourselves in the past – given good enough eyesight. But we are not really traveling to the past; we are watching a movie in space and viewing our image from the past. There is no sound in this film, and there are no past thoughts or feelings conveyed. If one supposes that thoughts and feelings are characterized by electrical signals in the brain, and these signals radiate along with the light beam, then, assuming we can receive them, one might argue that we actually were traveling to the past.

To muddle the mind further, consider that mass and energy don't only warp space, they also warp time. So time ticks at different rates depending on where you are – and certainly also on how fast you are traveling. And if that's not confusing enough, the latest talk on the block is that we don't really understand space and time at all – that they are allusions to a more fundamental reality. What we observe with our senses may have little to do with what is really happening.

Our consciousness appears to illuminate each moment in time before it moves on to the next moment, like the flow of a river. And we feel this flow. We sense the past upstream, the present here and now, and the future downstream. It's easy to drift downstream, but we can't seem to drift upstream. We call this the psychological arrow of time. But it's also the thermodynamic arrow of time. Remember the old saw about the egg that breaks on the kitchen floor but never puts itself back together again? Everything in the universe tends to become more disorderly with time, increasing a quantity we label thermodynamic entropy. Just relate that concept to a teenager's messy room. It never cleans itself up on its own. And if you clean that room to improve its appearance, it leads to even more disorder and increased entropy in the universe because of the energy expended in the cleanup. Maybe those teenagers do have a point in leaving their mess be.

Except for the existence of entropy, time could run backwards, and as far as the other laws of physics are concerned it doesn't matter one way or the other. Does time run backwards in other universes? Do other universes experience a different kind of time? No one knows – but we do know that when our universe reaches a state of maximum disorder, or maximum entropy, there will be no time, no past, and no present. Everything will be infinitely empty, infinitely homogeneous, and infinitely timeless. Nothing can happen. Nothing can change. The possibility of any further future would depend on quantum effects, just as it did at the dawn of our universe. But for now, time appears to flow onward, and everyone is dragged along with it. Observe a young child relishing life, oblivious to the flow. Look again, and that same child is old and bent. Life doesn't bother with the old and prefers to start anew. Natalie Clifford Barney got it right: "Youth is not a question of years: one is young or old from birth."

Cold and alone in the high mountains I tire of all this headwork. So I just let myself enter the universe – or perhaps, it enters me. I can unveil the universe at night. The sun tricks me during the day. I gaze for hours. I don't analyze. I don't think. I just let myself feel the universe. At this altitude, temperature, and dearth of man-made illumination, it is transparent. Unseen by most. There are so many stars. Sundry sizes, colors, brilliances. And some of these aren't stars at all, but galaxies. Are there other universes up there too, forbidden to me? I look at the dark spaces between the islands of light. Deep into those spaces. Further than my mind can go. And I know there's stuff there. But like the rest of it, it's inscrutable.

The ancients had a sense of the universe. They lived with nature and with the heavens. They knew the sky. They watched it breathe. They depended on it. We don't. We have our own lights. We have our own diversions. Our imagination is not whetted. We know all the equations but don't know the machine.

Primitive man had no understanding of the meaning of time. He did, however, notice the changing of the seasons. Eventually, he used the predictable movement of the sun to regulate his day. He noticed that shadows change in length and direction. First he used poles stuck in the ground, then monolithic pillars, and eventually he crafted crude sundials. Observing the phases of the moon gave him a more practical tool to track longer time periods. He relied on the heavens to sow and harvest, predict migration of animals, and prepare for winter. When he started wandering, he trusted the planets and stars. The Babylonians, at the center of Mesopotamian civilization, accurately noted the motion of astronomical bodies on clay tablets some 3500 years ago. They believed in a flat world, floating in waters of chaos, with a domed firmament. Some 1000 years later, the Hindus espoused cyclical universes with infinite universes existing at the same time. They may have gotten it right! Later cultures either concur with the cyclical model or opt for a static universe. Some of these universes are governed by reason, some by a god. Uniquely, the Pythagorean universe revolves around a central fire, while the Stoic universe is finite and surrounded by a void.

Our universe is going to have its 14 billionth birthday soon (that is, soon as in 200 million more years). At least we think that's her age judging by her looks, but she ain't telling. We only sense an infinitesimal portion of our universe through the radiation that has been traveling towards us since her birth. The stuff coming from the furthest expanses will never reach us. There, space is expanding faster than the speed of light. Some mysterious dark energy is shoving it. At least for now. And its negative! As this energy inflates into the nascent space, its density remains constant. That's sort of like watering down a bottle of 80 proof whisky and winding up with more whiskey, all at the same 80 proof. So this dark energy just keeps pushing objects in space further and faster apart. And in the process the negative energy of gravity increases (that is, it becomes less negative), balancing the freshly minted negative dark energy. And this flim-flam works because the total energy of the universe has not changed. In some googol years, when space is dark, cold, and empty, elementary particles will be eons of light years apart. Now for the record, the definition of a googol is the number 10 raised to the 100th power, that is the number 1 followed by 100 zeros (i.e. 10, 000, 000, 000, 000, 000, 000, 000, 000, 000, 000, 000, 000, 000, 000, 000, 000, 000, 000, 000, 000, 000, 000, 000, 000, 000, 000, 000, 000, 000, 000, 000, 000). Luckily, we have lots of time before we have to worry about being that cold, dark, and empty. And in case you're wondering about the spelling, the search engine Google meant to use the name googol, but accidentally misspelled it.

So, are we then back at the beginning? Effectively, at that remote time there would only be empty space, just as there was at the time of the Big Bang (except for the extremely high entropy – and we'll leave that quandary alone for now). Given enough time, there would be another quantum event leading to another Big Bang. Or, perhaps a collision with another brane. Or, some phenomenon we have not even imagined yet. Great for the universe, but not great for me. There would be no affirmation of me or my previous existence. I selfishly care about this because it was built into my genes.

I believe we've got reality wrong. Sure, we've got a few theories that are pretty reliable at explaining some of the chaos around us. But at the core, things are not what they seem. We think of 3 spatial dimensions when there may be 10. We think of time as liquid when it may be solid. We think of existence as matter when it may be energy. We think of substances as particles when they may be waves. We think of predictability when there may be unpredictability. We think of unique when it may be commonplace. Yet, we're lucky we can think rationally at all. Our thinking apparatus evolved for tasks such as avoiding predators, keeping out of the rain, finding food, and having a little sex. Evolution, working without a plan, did a poor job of engineering our brains. We often forget that evolution's only goal was to enhance the survival and propagation of the genes. It didn't worry about planning for future, more complex organisms like us.

Fortuitously, our brains are neuroplastic, and have been able to restructure themselves through cultural evolution. The cluster of neurons that once helped us aim a spear at a woolly mammoth now aims us to the moon and beyond. And here we are, using those same neurons to formulate classical mechanics, relativity, string theory, and quantum physics.

So, is reality depressing? It depends on your point of view and the crutch you choose to negotiate the journey. Regrettably for me, the answer is a resounding, yes. I cannot ignore the cold reality that has been exposed to me. I envy those that can. It would hurt less. My brain evolved to insure my survival, not to be truthful with me. I could swallow all the positive illusions my brain has prepared for me and ignore the accurate insights reality is unveiling. I could accept all the platitudes about the uniqueness of life, the opportunity to experience the universe, the chance to improve mankind's destiny. I could glorify in being part of the cosmic experience. I could accept the depression of reality while stealing bits of pleasure and gratification. I could cease to exist. I could find a god to worship.

Bertrand Russell said it well as early as 1923, without recourse to our current fund of knowledge: "That man is the product of causes which had no prevision of the end they were achieving; that his origin, his growth, his hopes and fears, his loves and his beliefs, are but the outcome of accidental collocations of atoms; that no fire, no heroism, no intensity of thought or feeling, can preserve a life beyond the grave; that all the labors of the ages, all the devotion, all the inspiration, all the noonday brightness of human genius, are destined to extinction in the vast death of the solar system; and the whole temple of Man's achievement must inevitably be buried beneath the debris of a universe in ruins – all these things, if not quite beyond dispute, are yet so nearly certain, that no philosophy which rejects them can hope to stand. Only within the scaffolding of these truths, only on the firm foundation of unyielding despair, can the soul's habitation be safely built."

IV   CONSCIOUSNESS

"Looking for consciousness in the brain
is like looking inside a radio for the announcer."
Nassim Haramein

The bad news is that our consciousness will cease to exist when we die, but we spin fables about its eternal presence. The good news is that part of that fable may be true.

Fine, but just what is consciousness, specifically self-awareness. Well, the current scientific account relates consciousness to the linking of brain cells, or neurons, to process information. When large numbers of these neurons fire synchronously in definite patterns, they form a correlated network whose state becomes consciousness. But how does that happen? No one knows, though a few researches claim that these states are simply mental representations – mental events symbolizing physical entities. Some areas of the brain only receive information from our sensory inputs and don't do much processing. Other areas, such as the cerebral cortex, connect many neurons together to produce rudimentary conscious thoughts. As more neurons are linked in complex patterns, more sophisticated thoughts can be generated. Our brains contain more neurons than the number of stars in our Milky Way galaxy, and we form over a million new connections every day, while the Milky Way fashions only about seven new stars in an entire year. There's a limit to the complexity, however, as interconnecting too many parts of the brain leaves no capacity for discrimination in the thought processes. It's like groups of people all embracing the same philosophy – there's no room for flexibility and creativity.

But where did the neurons in our brain come from? Well, it started long ago with bacteria. Protein chains within the bacteria acted like switches controlling the passage of electrically charged atoms through the cell walls. This process eventually allowed the bacteria to sense and react to the external environment. Over time, these protein chains evolved into neurons. When individual cells finally clumped into simple cell colonies, these nascent neurons communicated across cell membranes. After that, it wasn't long for synapses, the junctions between neurons, to appear and facilitate the transmission of information in primitive organisms.

OK. But this description is too much like the sommelier suggesting a wine that has wonderful color and depth, classic dryness with nuances of French oak and hints of blackberry, an earthy nose with smooth pomegranate tones, a silky, soft, rich tannin finish, all complemented by a textured, rounded mouthfeel. To which the diner says: "Yes, but what does it taste like?"

I know consciousness when I experience it – the constant inner chatter, the sense of presence, the emotional flavor of things, the feeling of what it is *like* subjectively for me. I even assume others possess it, though I really can't be sure. They might be programed androids or zombies indistinguishable from me – but not having inner consciousness. Androids are robots with flesh-like bodies designed by humans. Zombies, originating in Haitian tales, are mindless fictional creatures craving for human flesh. Since I assume I am not unique, I must assume that others are conscious and have intimate sensual perceptions as well. I can retrieve these introspective qualities, called "qualia", from my own immediate experience. Consciousness, our perception of qualia, must have a purpose or it would never have evolved in the first place. It must have given us some advantage over non-conscious creatures – and if that is the case, we should be able to distinguish between them and us. We *feel* things. The evolution of pain is easy to understand as it alerts us to potential bodily or psychological harm. Gratification in food, shelter, and sex adds to reproductive fitness. Pleasure in the arts organizes the chaotic world and keeps our phobias in check. Good art strikes a balance between structure (organization) and novelty (disarray). But why, for example, is there pleasure, in a sunset? Obviously, aesthetic pleasure must also have an evolutionary advantage. It has been proposed that contemplating the qualities of an object or scene develops perceptual skills. And these skills are important because they help us make sense of the world. As children we looked at simple things, as adults we need more complex patterns to hone our skills. All skills are developed by repetition. The brain rewards us with pleasure, which is obviously enjoyable, coercing us to perform the pleasurable act again.

I loathe having all my actions, beliefs, and now pleasures unmasked as another spiritless gear in the cosmic clock. I allow, for example, the argument that supplanting the mystery of the universe with knowledge of its workings greatly enhances its wonder. And I do marvel at its complexity. But I also miss the mystery. Nevertheless, watching the sunset, I am free to delight and pleasure in the experience, and leave the honing of skills to my subconscious.

Philosophers talk about the 'Easy Problem' and the 'Hard Problem' of consciousness. Of course, that is relative. There are no easy problems. Nicholas Humphrey writes: "Consciousness seems to be an impossible thing, because we cannot see how it could come from a material, physical universe. The 'Easy Problem' is concerned with the physical and biological mechanisms by which consciousness might be generated in the human brain. The 'Hard Problem', by contrast, is really an ontological problem—how to account for the experience of qualia at all in a physical universe. The mere existence of qualia and consciousness imply that the notion of a straightforward physical universe might be a tad naive."

Many philosophers agree that consciousness may be another fundamental entity of the universe, just like familiar entities of space, time, mass, and electric charge. And it may be universal, existing at diverse levels, not just turned on or off, depending on the organism or object. After all, most of nature exists in a continuum without discrete boundaries (quantum physics aside). What about rocks or bacteria? That's going to take a big leap of faith. Insects, and other small organisms may have some level of conscious mental state, but not self-awareness. Animals are another matter. We'll never know for sure, but apes, dolphins, killer whales, African grey parrots, magpies, pigs, elephants, and to a certain degree octopuses, exhibit behavior consistent with some form of self-awareness. We should not be too surprised. Charles Darwin, some 150 years ago, realized that "differences between species are differences in degree rather than in kind". In other words, if we possess consciousness, related organisms must also possess consciousness on some level.

Although brains are not in short supply, we humans are unique in the sense that our brain size, relative to our body size, is enormous. And brain size correlates with intelligence. Our multifaceted brains gradually enlarged over many millions of years, and then at a much faster rate during the last few million. This was probably related to our complex developing culture, language, and cognition.

Now the really hard one. Can machines be made conscious? That is, can *we* make machines that are conscious? Someone, something, already made *us* machines conscious. Can we build consciousness out of non-organic materials, or must we stick to the original organic stuff? Can we just copy all the brain circuitry we possess? Could such a machine feel? How would we know if we ever succeeded?

Computer simulation, as we will see later, is not consciousness. A computer uses only a few very fast processors at most. Our brain uses hundreds of billions of processors, our neurons, each processor connected to countless other processors. That's why computers are good at rote math, and we're (hopefully) good at personal relationships. Our brains are able to interact with the world on many levels.

Computers, using serial processors, will never be conscious no matter how fast or large we make them. The brain somehow produces consciousness using boundless parallel correlated networks. If we can build such a computer -- and we will -- it will be conscious. That machine, however, will be beyond a computer. Yet, it still won't be able to do anything. We need to amalgamate it with a very sophisticated robot which can interact with its environment. And the implications of all that are staggering.

If consciousness is indeed a fundamental entity of the universe, is it continuously being created just like dark energy? And if it isn't, is there enough of it to go around to supply inanimate objects as well as sentient beings – not just in this world but in the entire universe? And when inanimate object or sentient being "die", is consciousness recycled or do we get to keep it? Is it reserved for us before we exist and apportioned as we mature? Do our brain cells have preference if it is in short supply? Are clumps of consciousness prewired like brain cells? Do they possess the equivalent of DNA? Nonsensical questions like these often reveal great truths.

Conversely, Daniel Dennett and other materialists propose that consciousness is simply the virtual machine, *us*, becoming the object of its own perceptual systems. That is, discrete areas of the brain observe each other in a continuous feedback loop, and since they are all part of the whole, they experience the illusion as consciousness. Does consciousness then emerge from the complex interaction of fundamental processes, the whole being not only greater than the summing of those processes but different from those processes? Is consciousness just neural activity? Is it just an emergent property of the brain? Consider combining two chemical elements to create a compound having properties totally different from the original chemicals. Yet, the original atoms are still preserved in the newly created compound, albeit arranged differently. For example, take the highly reactive metal sodium, and the toxic gas chlorine, and combine them to form sodium-chloride, commonly known as table salt. Is this a genuine emergent property of the chemicals, or are we just interpreting the summation of the chemicals in more depth? To me, it seems a matter of semantics. An emergent property may seem enigmatic, but it is only another way of looking – and no laws of physics are violated, and no paranormal entities are summoned. In short, an emergent property is an elaborate way of articulating that the whole *appears* to be more than the sum of its parts. In truth, the whole is never more than the sum of its parts; there's no magic, it's just that we are not always able to consider the complex interaction of *all* the parts. So, the concept of an emergent property is useful, since it would be just as impractical to consider the interaction of all the parts, as it was to analyze the flight of a bee seeking nectar by analyzing every single atom involved in the process.

Is consciousness then just an emergent electro-chemical illusion of the brain? Well, if we are aware of the illusion and experience it – as we clearly do – then the illusion must be our reality. Alternatively, consciousness may only be a physical brain state, and the attendant qualia, "what's it like" feeling, may only be *that* physical brain state. Our brain then interprets that state as something non-physical, even though there is nothing non-physical there. We experience the same deception in a dream. There's no external action, only a physical brain state which deludes us into believing the experience. Yet both in the dream, and in the reality, there's something else going on. Feelings! And how do you explain *that* with brain states? When we reflect on our consciousness, nothing seems physical about it. Consciousness must be more than a brain state. But what is it that is conscious?

On the other hand, one might explain feelings with brain states after all. An emotion, which is just a physical bodily change, is triggered by internal or external stimuli. Perception, or neurophysiological processing of the stimuli, results in changing brain states. These mental changes are what we call feelings. So, we don't have to explain feelings in terms of brain states, because they *are* brain states. And by extension, so are qualia – though you'll get a lot of arguments on that one.

Another notion that's been advanced is that consciousness arises through quantum effects. I love that one, because quantum effects are always summoned to solve inexplicable mysteries. This controversial theory of consciousness posits that entanglement and superposition, discussed earlier, could play a role in consciousness deep inside brain neurons. What's curious about this approach is that consciousness, which we can't comprehend, is explained through quantum effects, which we also can't comprehend.

Whatever the mechanism, our understanding of the natural order of the universe is incomplete. So, consciousness may be all-encompassing, or an emergent property of the brain, or only a simple brain state, or some quantum flimflam. But, if what we experience as consciousness *is* a natural biological product of the brain, consciousness may be an undiscovered fundamental entity of our universe. It would be fun to add another conundrum to our universe – after all, we've recently added dark energy.

Though I obviously don't remember it, researchers tell me that as a baby I contained the entire universe, unaware of the boundary between me and the rest of it. Anything "outside" was either an extension of me or placed there for my personal pleasure. What a long way my ego was destined to fall. As a boy, I never thought about consciousness. I was the entire holistic package. Consciousness was not a separate entity to be dissected and analyzed. When I matured, I experienced consciousness as a fog enveloping and penetrating me. But it was still an indivisible part of me – like the soul that others espouse. I remember a time when I did believe in the soul, and it felt pretty much the way consciousness feels to me now, with the same impasse of connecting a non-physical entity to a physical one.

So, how could a non-physical entity such as consciousness, or the soul, be connected to a physical entity, the body. Plato believed the body shackles the soul until it is released upon death, only to be shackled again in another body – but gave no details of the process. Aristotle held that non-physical substances are just diverse forms of physical substances and are snuffed out in death. The great 17th century philosopher, René Descartes, deemed that the mind, which he equated with the soul, was indeed a non-physical entity, but was somehow connected to the physical body at the pineal gland near the center of the brain. This conjecture relates to one of the "Hard Problem" alternatives introduced earlier – substance dualism, the belief that consciousness is a fundamental property of the universe, different from a physical property. Another possibility, property dualism, points to consciousness as an emergent property of physical substances. There, are of course, other possibilities, but these two predominate.

And here, I need to rethink my past denial of dualism – the differentiation of body and mind – though not in the sense that an actual conscious entity exists on its own and envelops us in its aura, but that consciousness may be a non-physical feature of the physical brain. If such a duality exists, a connection exists, but our inherently limited brains may never be capable of comprehending the relationship. So, I'm torn between consciousness being an emergent property of a physical brain, and consciousness being another fundamental element of our universe – with apprehension of the latter, however, because it feels a little too "new age" to me. But, if I'm honest with myself, I must conclude that consciousness is only a brain state, and my brain is only modeling the reality of consciousness.

Although consciousness in our universe probably exists as a continuum, I choose to sort it into four broad categories. My views on this matter have expanded since my previous works, so I reiterate them here. The first category is the consciousness of things we would never consider as having consciousness: an atom, a virus, a bacterium, a stone, a tree. As we move up this scale, each succeeding example may have a few more "grains" of consciousness than the previous one. I have a hard time with this, but then I also have a hard time with quantum effects, multi-dimensionality, and just my own mere existence – so I'll keep an open mind on this for now.

The second, I label pre-consciousness, which is nothing more than highly developed instinct, innate biological traits not involving learning – the woodpecker hoarding nuts in hollows to retrieve again when needed, the duck hatchling following the first thing it sees when born, the dog shaking water off its coat. Third, is realization of oneself and the environment. Although this requires a critical brain size, it does not yet put the subject into the picture. Take the hound scheming how to procure his supper as he perceives the rabbit across the clearing. The hound knows about the rabbit, and he knows something about himself, but he does not know that he is a hound or that he is reflecting on the rabbit.

Finally, we have self-consciousness or awareness of self, which requires an even larger brain size, and perhaps some form of mental *symbolic* language – the gourmet delighting in his foie gras, and observing himself in his own delight; that is, putting himself into the picture. He understands he is delighting in his foie gras, but he also comprehends the fact that he understands. And maybe beyond all that, there is a fifth category: the universe being conscious of itself.

I can't grasp the idea of not having existed in the distant past, existing now in the present, and then not existing again in the remote future. I suppose it's because of my relationship, or perhaps lack of relationship, with time. I've had an incarnate past as far back as I can remember, I'm living in the present, and I can imagine a future with me in it. But what exactly exists at this moment? A collection of atoms I call "me" that chatter to themselves like an old senile person? Maybe that's all that exists.

So, where was I before I was born? That's another nonsensical question. It has its roots in the ego and the "I" that doesn't exist. Similarly, where will I be when I am dead? None of us wants to let go. We all picture our own funeral, listening at the secret grilled window as the Sultan's concubines listened to State secrets in 16th century Turkey. I had a friend, terminally ill, who planned her own funeral right down to the tea sandwiches and cookies she intended to serve. I'm sure she fully expected to respond personally to the ensuing sympathy cards.

Why am I only aware of my own mind? Could I have more than one mind in my body? What does it feel like for an epileptic person to have the two hemispheres of their brain severed? Do they have two minds? Do I have the same mind today that I had yesterday? What is my mind?

Well, my mind is either only a state of my brain, or an emergent property of my brain, or a natural biological product of my brain, which is just a physical organ of my body. My brain developed after conception through cell growth and eventually started observing itself, and that's what I'm experiencing now as a mind with conscious self-awareness. But other brains developed too, let's say Jane's brain. Her mind is aware of itself, but not aware of my mind, as I am aware of myself, but not aware of Jane's mind. So, what caused "me" to be inside my mind observing my mind, instead of being inside Jane's mind observing her mind? Why didn't I develop this consciousness in Jane's mind and in Jane's body? Well, of course, the consciousness I would have developed would be Jane's consciousness, and I *would* be Jane.

What if my consciousness could get inside Jane's mind? It would be an intruder. It would only be an observer. Even if I scrutinized every detail of her mind, I would still not have her consciousness because I would not be able to "feel" what it's like inside her mind. If, however, her mind could also observe my mind, forming a feedback loop, are we then self-conscious of each other? Neither mind being Jane or me, but some grander hybrid mind? In the end, it doesn't matter whose body and mind I'm in, because looking out at the world nothing would appear different, except as Jane, I'd be wondering why I wasn't in Marcel's mind.

Are our minds like computers before the internet evolved? Isolated machines in our dark caves, unaware of the sunlight? Does the internet generate an emergent property of linked computers? I'm sure it does. Can we likewise link our minds? Yes, but we have a lot of growing up to do first.

I grasp the concept of consciousness. I have delved into this before. But I run afoul of that great barrier, the ego, when it comes to my own personal consciousness. I accept that my consciousness is a state of my brain, or an emergent property of my brain, or a natural biological product of my brain, which is a physical organ in my physical body, which is the sum total of all that I am. But I keep trying to introduce a separate and distinct "I" within all that, even as I know there is no such separate and distinct thing. This "I" has been diversely characterized as mind-aura, soul, or spirit. Mankind has a genetically endowed conviction, probably a primal survival mechanism, manifested through the superego, the universal-mind, mythology, and religion, which detaches the personal "I" from the physical body. But once again, it's only a construct that we have fabricated.

Since the physical body is just energy cloaked as matter, it would be reasonable to postulate that consciousness involves universal energy. This notion becomes more plausible with the recent proposal that the universe may indeed contain more than ordinary and dark energy, but also conscious energy. Although I am only aware of my own consciousness, the consciousness in other minds may meld with mine into some universal whole. Is it possible that minds are aware of other minds, but our limited awareness of ourselves and the cosmos denies us the experience? Perhaps, unknowingly I sense everyone's consciousness, as everyone's consciousness senses mine. If Jane experiences pain, I don't experience her pain directly, but on another level of consciousness I *am* Jane (or she *is* me) and I *do* experience her pain. Maybe there is such a thing as cosmic consciousness, especially if consciousness turns out to be a fundamental entity of the universe as postulated. Perhaps one must traverse a new dimension, or a brane in our higher dimensional universe, or another universe to find out.

The biggest delusion is to assume that there is a distinct "I". Whether that "I" is a spiritual soul, a construct of the superego, or a scientific marker of convenience, matters not. There is no such thing as "I". There is only a collection of brain cells that have organized themselves in such a way that they are conscious of each other – or at least that groups of brain cells are aware of other groups of brain cells, which in turn, are aware of still other groups of brain cells. And so it goes in an endless feedback loop. This is what we label mind, this is what we label self-consciousness, and this is what we label "I". So the question "why is there me" has no meaning, because there is no "me" to begin with.

V   MEANING

"We are meat puppets leading meaningless lives
in a meaningless universe."
Ronald Bailey

Yet somehow, in spite of this epigraph, I tell myself that I can bring meaning to it all – if only while I exist. Surely, nothing in the universe can bring meaning to life except life itself. I am the only one that can give life meaning. As Ronald Dworkin queries: "Why can't a life also be an achievement complete in itself, with its own value in the art of living it displays". But that begs the question of why there has to be meaning to anything in the first place. Our minds have either been deceived or compelled to require meaning in our actions and in our being. This is probably another survival mechanism. Without this deception, we might have accomplished nothing and perished in the process. On the other hand, maybe things just are, and no meaning or purpose is needed.

And without meaning, are we then just like machines? That's not necessarily bad. A machine is just an assemblage of stuff that organizes and manipulates information to produce predictable functional results. We think of such a definition as pejorative. But a thinking, conscious, sentient machine has already been designed and constructed by evolution – and it works pretty well!

But we are not computers. A computer doesn't understand what it does. It doesn't feel. It doesn't know that it's a computer. Make it bigger, faster, more complex – and it's still just a computer. Our brains may operate like a computer, but a computer can't operate like a brain. It can mimic a brain, but a metaphor is not the entity. For instance, a computer can simulate the workings of the human digestive system, but try feeding it a pizza. If you overcome the obstacle of locating the pizza input-jack, it will still not delight in the smell, texture, and taste of the pizza – be it pepperoni or not. We machines are of a different quality.

But are we machines good? And what is good? And who decides? And does it matter? Well, to cut right to the chase, we machines are not good, never have been good, and probably never will be good. Sentient beings do not innately tend towards goodness. Not in this universe. Perhaps in other universes with other laws. But our universe has no morality, it just is. And our self-interest has been the prime evolutionary consequence of natural selection. Without an intervening power it could not be otherwise. Our love of kin, tribe, creativity, even spirituality, is all rooted in self-interest and thus dominance. We are the most violent, murderous, and cruelest machines known. Some of our excesses do not even seem to serve our self-interest (but, of course, they do). Yet somehow, we have developed a moral sense. No proof needed. We sense it inside, right alongside the "what's it like" feeling. Surely, another self-interest survival mechanism – but we can use it unselfishly for good. If we are willing. Can we depend on the most recently-evolved part of our brain, the frontal lobe of the cerebral cortex? After all, this is the brain's top executive, adept at organization and guidance of social behavior. Well, it hasn't helped us much yet. But if our civilization and our species are to survive, we'd better get busy. We are at the most dangerous stage of a civilization's evolution. We have mastered the technology of annihilating ourselves, but we have not yet mastered the art of living in harmony. I wonder how many civilizations on other worlds have already destroyed themselves.

Steven Hawking has some hope for us. He points out that although natural selection has brought us this far, significant changes in our genomes have taken many millions if not billions of years to occur. On the other hand, peripheral exchange of information through language can cause significant changes in human behavior in time scales of hundreds of years. Information available to us, however, has been growing at ever increasing rates. Preceding the 20th century it took about a century to double that information, by the mid-20th century it took some 25 years, and currently – one year! Our modern brains, which took some hundred thousand years to evolve from their primitive state, are not equipped to process the profusion of all this information. Hawking notes, however, that we will soon enter another stage of evolution where we will be able to alter our DNA. Should this come to pass we may yet moderate aggression and enhance our intelligence. We could eventually embody ourselves in intelligent machines based on mechanical and electronic components. Would I want to have my mind intermingled with the superior circuitry of such a machine? Would the machine even let me? Would there be a need for feelings and emotions? Would there then be enough intelligence to understand the universe? Would I even care at that point?

My greater fear is the possibility of having to live another life -- over and over again. Unknown, probably in an alien place, and in an alien form. My future consciousness would have no access to my past consciousness; otherwise, my present consciousness would be aware now. A notion that scares me as much, and seems analogous, is eternal life. I would have mastered everything. I would have experienced everything. I would have satisfied every intellectual pursuit, completed every task, eaten every favorite food an infinite number of times, sensed every pleasure, felt every emotional experience, and travelled to every patch of space –and then what would I do? There would be nothing left to accomplish, nothing to strive for, nothing to look forward to. It would be hell.

Sophocles had it right: "Not to be born surpasses thought and speech. The second best is to have seen the light and then go back quickly whence we came."

Our underlying perception of the laws of physics, as well as our concepts of how the universe works, are probably wrong, or at best so incomplete that they may as well be wrong. The "reality" we grasp does not represent what's really out there or what's happening out there. True, there are many mysteries that the human mind has been able to unravel, and many more it will certainly probe in the future, but I believe there are certain mysteries, such as the ultimate meaning of time, space, matter, and consciousness, that it will never fully understand because the human brain is not appropriately wired. We don't have the right cognitive equipment, and without explicit intervention, we are destined to remain that way. Our brains evolved to help us survive in the natural world, not to solve metaphysical problems. One might as well expect a cat to unravel the phases of the moon.

Classical physics is deterministic, that is events are causally determined by preceding events and natural laws. Theoretically, one could predict the outcome of any event based only on the position and motion of every atom in the previous event. As stated before, that implies that there is no such thing as free will. However, if consciousness were a fundamental entity of our universe, it would not fall under classical physical laws, and unless there were comparable restrictive metaphysical laws, would allow free will for sentient beings like ourselves. Another twist would be quantum physics, which suggests that the universe is not deterministic but probabilistic, adding a randomness factor. Hence, one could argue that our actions may not be fully predetermined by the universe, but rather tempered by randomness. Lastly, chaos theory (remember the butterfly effect) predicts that predictability is unpredictable at a practical level because of non-linear effects. It would take a computer larger than our universe, placed "outside" our universe, to calculate our precise future. And, of course, the output of that computer, being outside our universe, would not be accessible to us. If we could somehow put this computer, larger than our universe, inside our universe, it would just become part of the problem.

So, metaphysical consciousness, quantum physics, and chaos theory may give us some free will – or at least the illusion of free will. Even so, as I consciously choose a course of action that I intend to follow, it is already too late. My brain made the choice, unconsciously, before I even became conscious of it. And, the underlying choice may have been made almost 15 billion years ago by the universe. Granted, our "outside the universe" computer may be able determine my future course of action before I choose it, and thus I would have no free will, but nothing *in* this universe could have predicted my course of action, so in a sense I am acting with free will. I have free will based on my personal history, ambitions, emotions, and intellect – in other words, based on who I am, even if who I am was determined by past events. And, in spite of the shadow of random driven fate, it feels like *I'm* the one personally making the choice. Nonetheless, I know I can't trust my brain. It evolved to increase my reproductive fitness and pass my genes to the next generation. It's not concerned with truth, but with whatever will advance its agenda. I can't help wondering: "Have the gods tricked me yet another time?"

Pre-destined machine or not, I *am* alive. How do I define life? How do I categorize what is living and what is not? It's not as obvious as it appears. Philosophers and scientists have disagreed with each other for centuries. The Oxford English Dictionary, widely regarded as the accepted authority on the English language, quotes: "Life is the condition that distinguishes animals and plants from inorganic matter, including the capacity for growth, reproduction, functional activity, and continual change preceding death". But here, life is defined by the absence of death. Don't we define death by the absence of life? Can't there be life in things that are not in the animal or plant kingdom? Can't there be inorganic life? A more comprehensive perspective, as offered by theorists, is that "any definition must be sufficiently broad to encompass all life with which we are familiar, and must be sufficiently general to include life that may be fundamentally different from life on Earth. It may even be that life is not real at all, not a pure substance, but a process or concept instead."

On the other side of life is death. As Epictetus, that stoic Greek philosopher pronounced: "We should not fear death because we will not exist after death". So, we return to the familiar nothingness from whence we came. But that's bogus reasoning because we never existed before. We only came to exist in *this* life, so nothingness is an alien place. Further, we have to worry about the actual process of dying, per Woody

Allen's famous quip: "I am not afraid of death; I just don't want to be there when it happens." Does it hurt to die? Will my brain torment me with psychoses as it degenerates? I can handle all that, but not the loss of self. Does it help to rationalize that I, being matter, am just energy in flux – and at the moment that energy is aware of itself – and after my death that undifferentiated energy will continue to be part of the cosmos forever. Or better yet, that my conscious mind is not made out of matter, but out of some fundamental conscious stuff of the universe. No, it doesn't help because my ego is not fooled by the rationalization. Yet, irrationally – somehow – I love life in spite of it all.

I have arrived at an untenable position in my life. As a newborn I held the entire universe within me; now in my old age I grasp that I was never more than an encoded machine in an uncaring universe. Consciousness is an illusion of physical brain states. The universe is a mechanical structure destined for extinction. So, what am I doing here – and who is asking in the first place?

There are only two questions that concern me, and I've agonized about them before. "Why is there anything?" and "Why is there me – and why now?" Everything else is trite. True, space-time and energy can be generated spontaneously, especially given enough time (like eternity). However, if originally there was nothingness, then there would not have been any laws of physics, and specifically no quantum effects either, so space-time and energy could not have been created spontaneously. On the other hand, if I live in an ekpyrotic universe eternally cycling between birth and death, with no beginning or end, how do I wrap my mind around the concept of eternity? Would a true understanding of time, particularly that time is a construct and doesn't really exist, soothe my anxiety? I will not comprehend these mysteries with my current understanding of reality and my inadequate brain faculty. God – I wish there were a god to explain it all.

OK, but what about me? Why am I inside of me and not inside my dog? Why in this region of the cosmos and why in this time? Why not in the past, or in the future, or in another place, or in another body? Or best of all, why not never? The trivial answer, again, is that my natal cells proliferated, formulated a brain with electro-chemical circuitry, and with the help of social interaction developed a consciousness that recognizes itself as *me*. So I am left to ponder the message on the psychiatrist's answering machine: "Thanks for calling. Please tell me who you are and what you want. And if you can answer those two questions, you're way ahead of me".

So how do I live in this world today? I can glory in the beauty and complexity of the cosmos, mechanical or not. I can thirst for knowledge of its evolution. I can bring my own meaning to existence, even if that meaning has no enduring value. I can exercise whatever insignificant part of free will I control. I can marvel at my consciousness, which may be more than a physical brain state after all. And, I can hope that future sentient beings will gain clarity through a true understanding of fundamental physical and psychic

ABOUT THE AUTHOR

Marcel Fraser is married to Rebecca and lives happily in Santa Barbara, California. Mr. Fraser plays the piano and cello in amateur chamber-music groups and orchestras. He has released a CD of his piano music entitled "Selections from the Classics", and has taught piano and music theory. He has been President and on the Board of New Beginnings, a non-profit agency offering mental health programs to the community. His varied background includes managing his own real estate company specializing in estate properties. He had previously worked in the construction industry. Formerly on the scientific staff of MIT, he has also served as a bioengineering consultant at major hospitals, and has been associated with several research and development laboratories in Boston and New York.